P9-AOJ-294

THE LITTLE BOY
DOWN THE ROAD

THE LITTLE BOY DOWN THE ROAD

Short Stories & Essays on the Beauty of Family Life

Douglas W. Phillips

THE VISION FORUM, INC.
SAN ANTONIO, TEXAS

FIRST PRINTING
COPYRIGHT © 2008 THE VISION FORUM, INC.
All Rights Reserved

"Where there is no vision, the people perish." (Proverbs 29:18)

The Vision Forum, Inc.
4719 Blanco Rd., San Antonio, Texas 78212
www.visionforum.com

ISBN-10 1-934554-34-0
ISBN-13 978-1-934554-34-0

Cover Design and Typography by Justin Turley

PRINTED IN THE UNITED STATES OF AMERICA

To the little boys down the road
and in the tree who are not so little
any more, but who still wait for me:
Joshua and Justice

Other Books by the Author

The Bible Lessons of John Quincy Adams for His Son

The Birkenhead Drill

The Letters and Lessons of Teddy Roosevelt for His Sons

Poems for Patriarchs

Other Books from Vision Forum

Be Fruitful and Multiply

Family Man, Family Leader

John Calvin: Man of the Millennium

How God Wants Us to Worship Him

Missionary Patriarch

Of Plymouth Plantation

The Original Blue Back Speller

Reformation & Revival: The Story of the English Puritans

The R.M. Ballantyne Christian Adventure Library

So Much More

Ten P's in a Pod

Thoughts for Young Men

TABLE OF CONTENTS

FOREWORD
By Geoffrey Botkin

During a recent Thanksgiving holiday, a cynical American comedian introduced a gag on national television. It wasn't funny, but America laughed. The laugh was a nervous laugh. The skit had been conceived to be intellectual satire. Instead, it was a sad joke at the expense of the American family.

The show originated in New York City at the height of the holiday advertising season. The skit was built on this thesis: *The American family no longer exists except in dishonest, contrived imagery. So let's pretend with cynical style.*

The comedian mocked the family as a joke and men

as a caricature of manhood. With an air of cynical bravura, he suggested that men have a duty to keep the phony image alive—a duty to pretend to be "family men." He proceeded to show men how to do this with sentimental, artistic professionalism. Since the family and all family traditions are fake, he inferred, *go all-out when you fake your holiday greeting card*.

Get a professional photographer. Get professional models from a local modeling agency. Get a trim, blonde wife and two fresh-faced children. Get four festive sweaters that match and, "Ho, Ho;" the result is the perfect dishonest image of the outdated institution. "And don't forget to smile with toothy patriarchal insincerity!"

New York City is a media town. We've all seen New York's sentimental, artistic professionalism. Glossy magazines can spend six figures on one photo shoot in New York. We've seen, for example, elaborate Thanksgiving food features. The art director's assignment is usually a traditional one, of course. "Just make sure everything is family-centric."

The result can be a work of art. In the center of a massive family table is a memorable autumn centerpiece of pumpkins and Indian corn. An enormous roasted turkey reigns supreme over its lesser subjects: dishes heaped with steaming mashed potatoes, savory dressing and candied yams studded with pecans. Smiling aunts and grandmothers bring to the table cut crystal bowls of cranberry sauce and the Wedgewood gravy boat. The relatives crowd tightly 'round the table like a frame around an old master's painting. Some of these images are beautiful enough to bring tears to the eyes.

Could it be that we cry because everything in the glossy image is a prop in a New York studio? The smiles, the steam above the apple pie, even the glow from the family hearth—it's all fake, and we know it's fake. This is sentimental, contrived imagery.

However, it is also an attempt to recreate something that once existed. Americans would rather not pretend about family life. They would like to have it again. These desperate images of family life and a holiday table are based on historic reality, and even lonely art directors know this. Massive family tables were massive because families were once substantial. Heirloom platters exist because families were once multigenerational. Favorite recipes exist because families once met together—often—to enjoy real food. The family recipes still exist as historical evidence of a real homemaker. But what about the family?

The book you hold in your hands is about the historic reality of the family. Not just past reality, but the present and future historic reality of the family. This book is about the successful recreation of that reality in the present day. Not as image, but as substance. Not in mockery, but in honor. Not as fantasy, but as authenticity.

Twenty-seven years ago I met Doug Phillips' father Howard in Washington, D.C. Neither father nor son ever pretended to be family men. They *were* family men, and they were a rarity in that city. Doug was family-minded even then, as a faithful son in his father's home, learning things and observing things his peers never noticed about family life.

For many years I have watched Phillips family life with interest and respect. I have been a guest in Doug's boyhood home. I have been a guest in the home of Doug's manhood. I have been graciously seated, on Thanksgiving Day, at a real, massive, Phillips family table, set beautifully by Beall and the Phillips daughters, groaning under the weight of magnificent heirloom platters which overflowed with delicacies made from family recipes. I have marveled at the brimming abundance of good things that are real things. Authentic happiness, stimulating discussion, friends who wear genuine smiles, and domestic beauty in every direction. What I have seen surpasses the creativity of the best-paid art director. What I have seen is a real family in a real home.

This is because what Doug is building and fighting for

is substance, not image. What he now sees around him is reality. There are no props in the Phillips home, or in the life of Doug Phillips. None of his eight children came from a modeling agency. Doug treats each one as having come as a blessing from God, and it is this gratitude that has served him well as a strong creative force in all he is building as a sincere patriarch.

What you read in this book are the observations of a man looking squarely and thoughtfully and gratefully at the authentic family life that surrounds him. Doug sees these things as artists see light and poets hear metre. The book is a work of art. But it is not the contrived imaginings of a pretender or a man who sees fantasy inspired by reality. He is living the reality and learning from it, and now he is willing to share some of his most intimate observations with you.

What you will learn is that a glorious family is accessible to any man who will supply the courage and gratitude to build it, to preserve it, and then notice what has been wrought by the Authority who stands above every patriarch. Your own observations of your own growing family will prove to you that the family does exist and must exist as it was designed by God.

Families prove God's love for us. Families prove that our God is a God of patriarchal sincerity. God blesses families with beauty, and it is our privilege to see and observe the richness of history, blood, tradition, property, inheritance, daily love, hourly sacrifice, and present relationships. Families who see these things clearly will be able to fight effectively for the strength of the family in an anti-family culture, because they will have real families in real homes.

Geoff Botkin
San Antonio, TX
September 2008

INTRODUCTION

I am persuaded that the most beautiful, most important, and most life-changing stories are not found in the pages of newspapers, but in the everyday events in the life of the Christian family.

And that is the way it is supposed to be. The home is not only the incubator of life and the nursery of Christian culture, but it is the school of generational faithfulness from which the righteous man graduates. When the Bible paints the picture of the happiest men on Earth with the most far-reaching impact on history, it does so in the context of family life, meal time, and the blessing of children (Psalm

127, 128). That is why, when it comes to newsworthy events of eternal significance, nothing emerging from Hollywood, nor Washington, D.C., can hold a candle to the dining room table of a Christian household.

Sometimes the most important thing happening in the world is the couple deciding to adopt a baby, or the child honoring his mother, or the daughter repenting to her father. Sometimes it is a little boy who waits patiently down the road for his daddy to return from work so that he can simply hold the hand of the most important man in his life. These are the moments that really matter—the ones that will count in eternity. They are the everyday victories of the Christian life that will one day fill the heart of the old man with joy as he looks back on a life well spent. That is why, when the world has passed away, and the trends of this present culture are long since forgotten, those simple acts of love, done in the name of Christ and for His sake by a mother to her child, or a brother for his sister, will retain value with the saints in eternity.

This book is a short compilation of stories and essays about these moments. It is a book about the epiphanies of fatherhood. What do I mean? Every once in a while, the Christian experiences an epiphany—a moment when the scales are lifted from his eyes, and he really, really gets it—"It" being perspective on the most important things the Lord would have him to understand at that moment. These are moments of supreme clarity where he suddenly realizes—as if coming out of a slumber—the inexpressible preciousness of the Christian family and the unbounding love of Christ to shower sinful man with such earthly joys.

For me, these revelations have almost always occurred watching my family. In fact, I tend to have such epiphanies on two types of occasions. First, when the overwhelming beauty of God's gift of wife or children are laid before me in all of their dazzling glory through the "little things" in life—a baby in my arms, the blessing of a well-set family table, the consolation of my bride in times of difficulty, or the triumph of a son having faithfully executed the will of his father. Second, when I am reminded of the brevity of life, the fragility of human relationships, and my own utter dependence on the mercy of Christ to sustain and prosper that which I hold most dear on this Earth—my wife and children.

In the first part of my life, my happiest days were serving as a son to my father. In the second part of my life, my happiest days have been serving alongside my bride as a father to my children. *The Little Boy Down the Road* is a series of short stories and essays taken from these experiences as a son, a father, and a husband. Many of these stories are deeply personal. They are windows into experiences that have shaped my life. A sinful man, I too often forget the most important things in life. But these stories remind me of priorities like serving the Lord, honoring your father and mother, loving your wife, and shepherding the hearts of your children.

At the end of the day, the Christian warrior fights for two things. First, he fights for the crown rights of his eternal king, the Lord Jesus Christ. Second, he fights for his wife, his children, his family, and his household (Nehemiah 4:14). Only on these two grounds does he lawfully war for his nation. Destroy the family and the Church becomes an empty sepulcher. Destroy the family and the nation becomes dark and cruel. The purpose of this book is to help you remember the priorities of the warrior of the Lord. That is why it is my sincere prayer that this small offering of stories and essays will encourage you to do what I am still learning to do—to fight for my family, and to always remember the little boy down the road.

Persevero,
Doug Phillips
San Antonio, Texas

THE LITTLE BOY DOWN THE ROAD

Short Stories & Essays on the
Beauty of Family Life

CHAPTER I

THE LITTLE BOY
DOWN THE ROAD

Embracing a Father's First Priority

I have a little boy who waits for his daddy at the end of the street. For several years, we lived at the end of a long Texas country road. Every evening when I was away from home on business, my little boy would ask permission of his mother to take his little black and brown dog and his daddy's blackthorn walking stick to make the half-mile journey from the house to the picket fence which marked the beginning of the dirt driveway.

One day, I was delayed in my business. Some seemingly all-important grown-up concern distracted me. I forgot about the faithful little boy down the road who might be waiting for his daddy.

On my way home, the floodgates of heaven opened. For several minutes, the rain was so thick that I could not see ten feet in front of me. All I could think of was finishing my journey and getting out the rain. Finally, the downpour began to abate. It was only a drizzle by the time my car turned the last corner and approached the final street between me and a warm home and nice meal.

But in less than a fraction of a second, my business priorities, my concerns, and my grown-up thoughts would fade and vanish.

There was my little boy. He was holding a rickety umbrella in one hand, a walking stick in the other, and was wearing the biggest and most beautiful smile ever to grace the face of a little boy.

As I stopped the car and opened the door, he ran into my arms and held me long and hard. He was wet and shivering, but he never mentioned the rain, nor the hour-long wait that I later discovered he had endured just to greet his father. He simply said, "Daddy, I missed you. I am so glad you are home."

All afternoon he had been thinking of one thing: his daddy. He had lived for the time he could make the journey to the end of the road and for that one moment when he would run into my arms and tell me he loves me. Like the dog beside him, his devotion and faithfulness would not even be broken by even a tardy father and a rainy day. His day and his world revolved around that one moment when he could say to himself, "I am with my daddy again."

One day we moved to a wonderful new home provided by the Lord for a special season in our lives. The little boy down the road is a little bit less little. We no longer have a long country road. Now we have a giant tree. It is often beside that tree that my little boy waits for me now, sometimes with his regiment of brothers and sisters, now old enough to venture beyond the castle walls of our home.

The tree is adorned with climbing ropes, with occasional buckets hanging off the limbs, and with the many markings of boys who thrill and delight to climb and conquer the kingdoms of trees. In the evening time, we sometimes have what we call "tree time." This is a special thirty minutes when Daddy and sons climb into the tree and just talk. It's a time for stories, for imagination, and for just being boys in trees.

But I have never forgotten the rainy day and the little boy and his dog. Often, perhaps a thousand times, my mind has wandered back to that scene. Like all events in our lives, it happens once and must be savored and treasured.

3

I think it was this day that I grew to understand what it meant when Jesus said that true Christianity is having the faith of a child. The evidences of this faith are simple love, unfeigned loyalty, and the passion—the all-consuming passion—to be with the Father.

How thankful I am that our Heavenly Father will never be distracted, lose perspective, or switch priorities away from His beloved sons. He will not leave us waiting, nor will He need rain and storms to refocus His attention on us.

Oh God, help us to be more like You, to have the simple faith of our children, and to understand that, more than anything else, our children crave a relationship with us, even as You crave one with each of Your children.

Someday my little boy won't be waiting at the end of the road. Someday he won't ask me to climb "our" tree to hear Daddy stories. Someday the wonders of bugs and butterflies will be exchanged for the dreams of noble manhood. Someday we will discuss what it means to love a woman. On yet another more distant day, we will look at new life and discuss, not only as father and son, but as friends, the joys of raising children for the glory of God. Perhaps even someday, we will live to see our children's children walk in the grace of the light of God.

All of this by God's grace and mercy. But for now, my little boy still likes to climb trees, to snuggle in the great big chair, to hug, and to wrestle on the ground with his five-foot-eight father, who, for just a few more years, appears to be an insurmountable giant. What a gift! What a gift!

You may not have a little boy down the street, but perhaps you have a little girl looking out the window, or a baby in the crib, or a young man on the phone. Whatever gifts of life God has given you, and in whatever stages of their lives you find them now, remember that this season is a gift from God which lasts for but a moment and will then be gone forever. Have the faith of a child.

The message of life is relationships. Don't leave the little boy down the road waiting for long.

CHAPTER 2

THE WOMAN WHO CHOSE LIFE

*How Courageous Childbirth
Changes the World*

Forty years ago, a very courageous woman chose not to abort her baby. Unlike many unwed mothers, this woman had been previously married. She had borne sons and daughters. She had helped to raise a family. But now in her forties she found herself divorced and with child— the fruit of a brief immoral relationship.

If she was like other unwed mothers facing the challenges and stigma of an unplanned and unwanted pregnancy, she probably suffered from fear and disappointment. And I can only imagine the pressure she felt to try to erase the embarrassment, to end the physical discomfort, and to avert the potential shame and rejection she would experience as she faced her own legitimate children and extended family with the news that she had conceived a child with a married man.

In those days, abortion had yet to be legalized in America—that would come five years later. But even in 1967, it was readily available. It was the quick-fix of choice for any and all who wanted to run from life.

Perhaps it was because she had already experienced the power of motherhood. Perhaps it was because she understood that abortion is the merciless shedding of innocent blood. But whatever the conscious reason for her decision, I know that behind the stated reason was the remarkable grace of God.

And by God's grace, this courageous woman did not give in to her fears. On what may have been the most important decision of her life, she chose wisely. She determined that she could not kill her unborn child. She chose life.

Then, on October 6, 1967, a little baby came into the world.

Shortly after her birth, the newborn would be given to a woman whose name is now lost to history, but who would rock and nurse her for six weeks until the little baby was placed in the loving arms of a caring, adoptive family.

As a child, the little baby whose mother chose life would hear the stories of how Baby Brown Eyes was given to Daddy Blue Eyes and Mommy Green Eyes by a loving God who sets the solitary in families.

She heard these stories and many others. And the little baby whose life was spared grew. She grew into a woman, and one day God gave her a baby of her own—and then eight others, including one whose soul was taken to live in eternity.

That little baby would grow up to minister to unwed mothers. She would encourage untold numbers of adopted children to be grateful, content, and rejoicing in their circumstances because of the beautiful picture of spiritual adoption represented by their special, God-ordained placement in the homes of families that longed for them.

In fact, the little baby whose mother chose life would become a thriving woman—a beautiful Christian lady with a heart full of gratitude. And this dear lady would fill her years to the brim with such overflowing life and love that this one soul would profoundly touch the lives of men, women, and children, influencing thousands with the message of the beauty of Christian womanhood, the blessing of the fruit of the womb, and the hope which is only found in God, the One true Giver of life.

And that lady is my wife.

I was only two years old when a courageous woman chose not to abort the baby who would become Elizabeth Beall Phillips. And now, for the fortieth birthday of my beloved *esposita*, I want to give praise to the Lord Jesus Christ for His mercies in crafting and giving to me a remarkable woman who knows from the depth of her soul that life is God's precious gift, and that, but for His amazing grace, she would have been one of the forty million American babies who never survived the bloody dagger of the abortionist.

And I want to thank God for the grace that He placed in the heart of a scared but courageous woman who chose life.

Because she chose life, other babies have been born—some of whom would have been yet another horrifying abortion statistic had not their unwed mothers heard a message of hope from a Christian lady who was once a baby to an unwed mother herself.

Because this woman chose life forty years ago, I have enjoyed fifteen years of the happiest marriage for which a man could hope.

Because she chose life, I am surrounded each morning by eighteen loving arms—and I daily enjoy the kisses of nine precious sets of lips.

Because she chose life, hundreds (perhaps thousands) of daughters, wives, and mothers have been touched, encouraged, and given hope by the ministry of the very baby she gave life and then gave up. Because she chose life, there are souls who have been led to Jesus Christ as Lord and Savior and now enjoy the promise of eternal life.

Because she chose life, I have learned what it means to be deeply and desperately loved by a woman. I have experienced the joy of being a man whose wife delights in being a helpmeet suitable for me. I have drunk deeply from the font of happiness that comes to those who are blessed with life-mates who radiate contentedness.

Just before her death, the birth mother of Elizabeth Beall Phillips corresponded with the daughter she had never known. From the little baby she had only held in her arms for moments, this woman heard about the love of Christ. She discovered that the once-little baby had prayed for her year after year. And she found out that the baby she had birthed became a contented adoptive daughter who never doubted the goodness of God in placing her in a new home, and who enjoyed the happiness which comes from being loved.

I never met the woman who gave birth to my beloved. And I never will. But because she chose life, I am a happy man.

On behalf of grateful children and husbands everywhere who daily enjoy the blessings which came from the fruit of sorrowing mothers who chose life and the adoptive parents who gave homes to lost babies, I give praise to the Lord Jesus Christ, and I thank you, Clarice, for choosing life.

CHAPTER 3

THE ART OF HOME SCHOOL OPERA

The Blessing of Family Eccentricities

If you listen carefully enough, you can hear the sound of children singing. They are singing home school opera. At least that is what I hear at the Phillips' home. And it is music to a father's ears.

You have never heard of home school opera? Let me help you out.

But first I need to tell you a story.

The Phillips family is comprised of two types of vocalists—the musically inclined, and the essentially tone-deaf. The first group got their genes from my mother, and the second from my father.

When you put these two groups together, it gives new meaning to the expression "make a joyful noise unto the Lord." But we not only live with it, we love it.

My mother loves beautiful music. She loves Brahms and Pavarotti, and she taught her children to love them, too. I once asked Mom a somewhat odd and disturbing question, "If you had to make the choice between losing your sight or losing your hearing, which would you choose?" She never hesitated, "Oh, that's easy. I would much rather lose my sight. I couldn't bear to lose my hearing."

That left an impression on me. I am a book guy, and I think I would choose the opposite. But it told me a lot about my mother's commitment to beautiful sounds.

My father loves music too, but more the musical theater kind—joyful, boisterous, and full of zip. And he takes such delight in singing the lyrics. I think I knew the soundtrack to *Fiddler on the Roof* and *Oklahoma!* before I left my mother's womb. As a boy, I loved to listen to my father sing, and it never bothered me that he was notoriously out of tune. Dad actually reveled in the reaction he always got from his family whenever he would sing one of his out-of-tune songs—which was all the time. My dad's songs made me laugh. They made me happy because my dad was always happy singing them.

And certain tunes are still floating around in my head, like my father's morning wake-up song that began, "When I get dressed, in all my best, there are no flies on me."

I have been singing my father's song for forty years. But it hit me for the first time the other day—I have been singing it off-key because that is how I thought it was supposed to be sung. I realized this when I was trying to teach the "No Flies On Me" song to my children, and a member of the musically-inclined part of my family respectfully asked the obvious question, "Is it supposed to sound that way, or is that how Papa likes to sing it?"

I decided then and there that the song should not be fixed. It was a reminder of one of my father's most loveable eccentricities, and I wanted my children to be able to enjoy it. I predict that three generations from now, somewhere in the distant twenty-second century, some Phillips children will be learning the "No Flies On Me" song, singing it off key, and loving it.

The Blessings of Family Eccentricities

Large families tend to have large personalities. This is a good thing. It is good to have a household filled with life, and even more so when eccentricities are a reflection of the unique personalities and histories of families attempting

17

to persevere before the Lord.

I think family eccentricities can be a glory to the Christian household. They mark out each family as unique in the community of saints. They remind us that we are our father's sons and our mother's daughters. They bring humor to our lives and much-needed color to the body of Christ.

If you look closely at the families in your local church, you may notice that some of the strongest Christian families have the most self-evident eccentricities. Perhaps it is the way they walk, or laugh, or pronounce certain words. Maybe it is the way they decorate their home, the unique diet they embrace, the books they read, or the subjects they most passionately discuss.

All families have eccentricities, but large families tend to showcase those eccentricities just by virtue of their sheer number. I love to see a household filled with children, each with a unique personality and unique gift, nonetheless displaying their common denominators as members of a particular household. Welcome diversity within an environment of unity is a key component to family prosperity. The bigger the family is, the greater the potential for a division of labor and gifts. A division of labor and gifts means strength to the household. Wise parents seek to perpetuate the blessed distinctions between each child while cultivating two things: first, a common faith; second, a common family culture, rife with eccentricities unique to that family.

You can look at pictures of my sons and me going back for more than a decade. Here is what you often will see: If I wore funny hats, they did too. If I wore special pins, they would want to do the same. When I wore suspenders, they would also. And they did not do this because I asked them to dress a particular way, but because they wanted to be like Daddy. For years, I have been asked—almost daily—"Daddy, what will you be wearing today?" I never get tired of hearing this question because it means that, for one more day, the Lord has placed it on the heart of my child to identify with his eccentric, sinful father.

I am also convinced that the more that children of Christian parents distance themselves from the unique look and feel of their own families, the more they limit their potential as multigenerational visionaries. It is a sad social commentary on the state of the modern Christian family that so many children are exchanging the blessing of family eccentricities for the curse of peer conformity. They prefer the look, gait, and spirit of the children of the world to the unique expressions of identity found in the Christian family.

There are two significant ways parents contribute to

this problem. The first is by minimizing the importance of Christian family culture. Families that don't eat together, read together, pray together, and worship the Lord daily in the home together usually have a negative Christian family culture. Home is more of a flophouse. There is nothing inspiring about a flophouse.

The second way parents contribute to the wandering vision of their children is by allowing their sons and daughters to make large investments of time in social groups that steal their hearts. The Bible says, "Where your treasure is, there will your heart be also" (Matthew 6:21). Time is one of the greatest treasures that any child has. Invest the time-treasure of a child with negative peer influences, and that is where his heart will be. A culture of family fragmentation and peer influence is a culture that promotes dishonor. It is not surprising, therefore, that the sitcoms of our present day train children to mock their parents and to distance themselves from the eccentricities of Mom and Dad.

Christian family culture is an antidote to such dishonor. This means building homes full of living and full of eccentricities. Eccentricities reflect strengths, weaknesses, and often both. Both are important for the life of the Church. Both make our loved-ones—well, more loveable. From the strengths, we learn character.

From the weaknesses, we learn to have compassion for our brethren. Both are important components to the community of fallen, sinful men and women called the Church. I am convinced that, as we look back on the lives of our family, we will remember with much satisfaction the happy eccentricities that became the spice of our family life.

Understanding Home School Opera

The Phillips family has many quirks and eccentricities. Here is one—we are loud. Sometimes, we are really, really loud. We often call ourselves "The Loud Family." Families that come to our home expecting perfect order or peace and calm as a representation of our "true spirituality" will be sorely disappointed.

Here is what they should expect: the grunts of children wrestling and sword fighting; hoots of laughter as boys and girls play with adorable toddlers; wild tickle-fests that result in uncontrollable squealing; little girls dancing; the never-ending sounds of legions of hamsters spinning on hamster wheels; dogs woofing and cats meowing; babies crying; and hearty cheers around the dinner table for Momma after a delicious meal.

Then there is the ethnic component to "The Loud

Family." Add a couple thousand years of accumulated Jewish *chutzpah*, and at least a few hundred years of Irish blarney, some Russian drama, Southern enthusiasm, and Northern ingenuity, and you will meet a band of pure-bred mutts with a clever, dramatic approach to making very loud sounds a happy component of our family culture.

But one of the most unusual eccentricities of the Phillips' home is that, if you show up at just the right time, you may have the privilege of listening to one of my very favorites sounds of family life—home school opera.

The leader of our home school opera ensemble is a little songbird by the name of Faith Evangeline.

Faith Evangeline is a little wisp of a thing that floats around our home on gossamer wings. She is so light and ethereal that I sometimes ask her if she is going to float away from her daddy and fly off into the sky. So I call her my "fly away, fly away sweetheart" and ask for butterfly kisses whenever she is near.

But God has given this little girl an unusually strong set of pipes. Boy, does she love to use them. She uses them in her room, in the car, in the shower, in the kitchen— pretty much everywhere. She constantly fills the home with song—songs familiar and songs unknown to anyone but Faith Evangeline.

And my favorite songs that she sings are home school opera.

How can I describe home school opera?

Here is what I want you to imagine: Take a famous aria—"O Sole Mio," or perhaps "Climb Every Mountain" from *The Sound of Music*. Now add words—not actual rhythmic lyrics, but words about everyday life.

Here is an example, set to "O Sole Mio."

"I...am...cleeeaaaning the k-i-tchennnn!
I am doing it for Moooooommmmeeeey!
I am cleaning the kitchen
Because she told me soooooooooooooo...
Virginia's crying, crying in the kitchen
I think I'll help her, Oh yes, I will!"

To get the full sense of Faith Evangeline's unique home school opera performance style, it is crucial that you sing it in falsetto, at the top of your lungs, using highly exaggerated vibrato. Here is another example, set to "Climb Every Mountain":

"Feed every hamster; Feed every one.
Feed every hamster; feed them till you're done."

The core of home school opera is singing about family life. Whatever you are doing at that moment—sing about it. Sing about it passionately. And let the whole house hear you sing about it.

Since the lyrics to home school opera are made up on the fly, it is difficult to have others sing the same song with you. But that shouldn't stop them from singing home school opera—simultaneously with you!

Done well, this can really be an Olympic exercise in the preciousness of family cacophony. Home school opera beginners dare not try more than one soloist at a time, but as they move from junior varsity to varsity, it is not uncommon to have multiple vocalists singing simultaneously.

It is really quite an experience.

On a good day in the Phillips family, one might hope to hear as many as three or four soloists performing home school opera simultaneously: There might be Faith Evangeline singing from the depth of her soul about her studies or chores—and doing so at a decibel range that would make a Wagnerian soprano proud! Just a few feet away one might find Providence singing songs about pirates and toy soldiers. Near him, Jubilee might be humming about the Scriptures she is reading. On the floor you might see our toddler, Virginia, repeating the one line she can remember from her favorite hymn about the holiness of God—"Hoowey, Hoowey, Hoowey . . . Loooor God Amightey...Hoowey, Hoowey, Hoowey!"

Please note: When calculating the level of difficulty of home school opera performance in your home, it does not count as an additional soloist if one of the older children joins in by singing, to the opening melody of Beethoven's *Fifth Symphony*, "Please stop it now! Please stop it now!"

It is true that not everyone appreciates the fine nuances of home school opera to the same extent that the daddy of the Phillips' home appreciates it. But everybody recognizes that home school opera is a truly unique and colorful contribution to the musical culture of "The Loud Family."

Home school opera is music to this father's ears. It doesn't have to be lyrically strong. It does not have to rhyme. And in our family, it does not even have to be in tune.

It does have to come from the heart—which is the only type of home school opera I have ever heard. It is an eccentricity of the Phillips family, and I am good with it. I am good with it because, from my perspective, there are few things as precious in the culture of the life of the Christian household as the glory of a boy singing the ballads of family life, or a girl making melody in her heart to the Lord.

Fatherhood and the Sounds of Life

Every day there are thousands of sounds competing for the attention of fathers.

There is the sound of the television set. This is the intoxicating call of the ancient siren, lulling men to slumber, urging them to check their brains at the door of their homes and float into a sea of passivity until they crash upon the rocks of life. There is the sound of the city and the business world. These sounds sometimes give men the false assurance that corporate success is the true test of manhood.

Then there are the diverse sounds of the world in general—a never-ending barrage of sound coming from the hum of machines, the chatter of people, and the background music that follows modern man from elevators to his car to the local coffee shop. These sounds remind us that we are not alone. But they also train us to be incapable of sitting in silence and communing with our God. Like a drug that takes away the pain of life at the expense of the clarity of the mind, these sounds often fill our heads with unnecessary distraction, such that it is a struggle to focus on the most important things.

We live in a world of sound pollution—too much sound, all the time. We spend so much time listening to indiscriminate sounds that we often fail to hear the music of life. We need to reduce the pollution and start listening to the most important music—the sounds that make a Christian household a Christian household.

There is music in the sound of a family worshipping the Lord together. There is music in the sound of babies laughing, of children studying at the family table, of sisters preparing meals for their family, and of moms reading bedtime stories to little ones. When these sounds truly reflect hearts that long to please their Heavenly Father, they make up the aroma of a life well-lived before the Lord.

Of course, the most beautiful music to a father's ear are any sounds which allow him to experience the blessing of watching his children walking in truth. On this point, Jesus Christ, the author of Holy Scripture, wrote, "I have no greater joy than to hear that my children walk in truth" (3 John 1:4).

Conclusion

I am persuaded that the sounds of a household are a window into the soul of the family.

For most American families today, the sounds being projected are filled with the noise pollution of the television or even with the discordant shouts of family turmoil. In other cases, the modern household is an empty tomb—a shadow of what family life was meant to be. In these households, there is little sound because there are no children. Or perhaps the silence stems from years of family fragmentation in which mother, father, and children each have their own individualized lives largely lived out far from home.

The Christian household is meant to be different. It is a place of love and living.

And that means noise. It means houses filled with the glorious echoes of babies crying, of children playing, of mothers teaching, of fathers training, and even a few animals chirping, meowing, or woofing. It means life—with all of its glory, sadness, and joy. It means happy homes of highly eccentric families, each with their own unique vision, style, personality traits, and expressions.

These homes are not museums. That means they are rarely immaculate. Gloriously organized chaos is sometimes a more apt description. They are homes made up of grateful and forgiven sinners who recognize that there is no greater joy than to daily experience the nobility of the commonplace, from the simple disciplines of Christian life—prayer, studies, work—to the thrill of watching fathers eating the fruit of their labors, of moms who radiate the glory of being fruitful vines, and of brothers and sisters who gather around the family table like precious olive plants (Psalm 128).

Look for these households. For their number is growing. They are part of a great spiritual work where the hearts of parents are turning to their children and children to their parents (Malachi 4:6). And when you find them, listen. If you listen carefully enough, you may hear the sounds of little children singing. They will likely be singing psalms and hymns and spiritual songs, or perhaps even the sweet refrains of nursery rhymes and childhood ditties.

But for my taste, there is no sound as exalting to the spirit than the sometimes melodious, but always enchanting, lyric exclamations of little ones engaged in the sacred art of home school opera.

Give unto the LORD the glory due unto his name: bring an offering, and come before him: worship the LORD in the beauty of holiness. (1 Chronicles 16:29)

CHAPTER 4

THE ANIMAL FAIR

*What We Learn from a Child's
Relationships with Animals*

For many children, the first love affair of their life is with a pet.

To deeply love an animal is to experience a special kind of romance reserved exclusively for the journey of childhood. It is an experience that cannot, will not, and probably should not be repeated the same way in the world of adults. For a brief season of life, it is possible for a child to feel the wonderful and mysterious joys of giving their heart to an animal—"puppy love," so to speak.

This is different than the love a little girl has for her daddy, or a son for his mother. On the other hand, the relationship between a child and a pet is a shadow of the love that a parent has for his child. Think about it this way—there is always the potential for profound emotions whenever one person becomes accountable for the life of another. When a little boy owns his first dog, or a girl her very own horse, they are immediately vested with previously unprecedented responsibility. The well-being of that animal depends on the discipline, provision, and love of the child. In reality, it is sometimes a child's first significant act of dominion as he personally exercises authority over one of God's creations (Genesis 1:28).

Of course, it is quite healthy for children to raise animals without becoming emotionally attached. The care of livestock is the classic example. Wise parents teach their children to understand that the primary mission of such animals is to produce food for the family and to increase the wealth of the household.

But it is different with a pet. A pet becomes more than just another animal. It is a comforter, a playmate, a boon companion, and sometimes even more. Sometimes, it is a loyal defender.

The Family Zoo

I went to the Animal Fair,
The birds and the beasts were there;
The big baboon by the light of the moon
Was combing his auburn hair.

You should have seen the monk,
He sat on the elephant's trunk.
The elephant sneezed and fell on his knees,
And that was the end of the monk.

Pets tend to accumulate.

Children know that, once the door has been officially opened to bringing alternative life forms into the house, the only issue left to resolve is how many and how fast. But there is an added incentive for pet accumulation in the home school family. Animals are not just companions—they are research projects. At least, that is a plausible argument to present to Dad when making the case for the Blue-tongued Skink you hope to add to your bedroom menagerie, or the baby bird you rescued which is temporarily living in the Lego® castle you made for it.

After more than two decades getting to know families in the modern home school movement, I have come to believe that they represent some of the most hardworking, committed, and caring people in all of Christendom. But when it comes to animals, there are two types of home school families—those who exclude pets from their homes, and those who turn their homes into zoos. There is nothing in-between.

We fall into the "turn their homes into zoos" category.

From rabbits to goats, tarantulas to chickens, dogs, horses, cats, fish, cows, crabs, birds, reptiles, vultures, and even baby deer—at some point or another, they have all lived with, besides, and even on top of the Phillips family.

There was Bambi, the diaper-wearing, eternally-whining fawn that lived in our home for three months and was a frequent guest at our dinner table. She followed the children wherever they went, including long walks. Until one day Bambi decided it was more fun to play with grown-up deer than young children. Bambi was eventually replaced by another fawn we named Flag, whose toes were painted with pink nail polish by the children in the hope of identifying her if she ever joined Bambi.

Of course there were fish—and strange ones too. At one point we played mother to a strange eel-like fish and a shrimp that was constantly shedding and eating his own exoskeleton to the horror and delight of my children. There was the cantankerous, but charming, thirty-two-year-old racehorse, Mr. M.L., who lived with us for the last two years of his life. Rising early in the morning each day to muck his stall and put liniment on his legs as he would whinny contentment and gratitude taught us the blessing of compassion for God's creatures. There was his less-loveable side kick with a side kick, Amos the pony. There was Moses the calf. There were the docile bats we could pick off the barn walls, and the barn cats that might as well have been tigers for their ferocity towards humans.

Along the way there were more than a few felines, including a beautiful fluffy white cat named Snowball. She was a rescue animal, but despite her humble origins, Snowball thought she was the Queen of Sheba. We talked about her as a model of the type of vanity our little girls should avoid. We reminded our daughters that "as a jewel of gold in the snout of a swine, so is a beautiful [cat] that lacks discretion." Eventually Snowball made the point for us. Within weeks of our family moving to a new neighborhood, Snowball decided to exchange our family—the one that rescued her and loved her despite her conceited behavior—for a more upscale household with a higher standard of living, plush sofas, and gourmet cat food. Apparently, Snowball had been sneaking out of our home and interviewing different families in the neighborhood for the position of owner. When she found an owner capable of caring for her in the elite manner which she deemed acceptable, she just moved in. Every once in a while, Snowball would emerge from her new lair just long enough to sun herself or meow out orders to some other sycophantic neighborhood cat. The children would see Snowball from time to time, but she never acknowledged them again. Shocked by this flagrant display of feline disloyalty, we began thinking of her less as the Queen of Sheba, and more as the *Cruella De Vil* of the neighborhood cat mafia. But there was an upside. The new turn of events furnished Dad with many nights of creative storytelling. To this day, when the neighborhood raccoons plunder our trash or eat the chow left out for our pets, we wonder if these bandit-browed thieves are simply stoolies in the employ of the true mastermind of catdom—Snowball.

Dog Tales

Dogs are another story altogether. We have had twenty-one of them—twenty-one!

That number includes puppies, dogs we adopted,

dogs that adopted us, dogs we eventually gave away, and four fatalities—one of which was a defining event in the life of our family.

To quote Julie Andrews—"Let's start at the every beginning, a very good place to start."

Long before there was the Doug Phillips Family, there was a little seven-year-old boy named Douglas. On February 24, 1972, I was on a long walk with my dad through my neighborhood in Fairfax County, Virginia, when I found myself looking into the big brown eyes of a rust-colored, tail-wagging puppy.

It was love at first sight.

But the pup had no collar. No tag. Who owned him?

After appealing to my dad to help me find answers, he inquired of a local homeowner. We were informed that the puppy had been thrown out of a car and left to die by the side of the road.

That was all I needed to know. Everything became incredibly clear. I had one mission—take that dog home and devote my entire boyhood to loving it. That dog needed a boy, and I knew a boy who needed a dog. It loved me, and I loved it—what else was there to talk about?

To get the dog, I had to appear before Mom—the Phillips family equivalent of the Supreme Court for all matters pertaining to pets. Dad was, without question, the chief executive of the Phillips family house. Of that, there could be no doubt. But when it came to animals, he appointed Mom as the court with original and final jurisdiction. Up to that moment in history, the court had ruled in the negative on all previous appeals for animals. Exceptions had been granted for small, aquarium-sized turtles, but that was it. Dogs and cats were out. The court found that they were contrary to the "general welfare clause" of the Phillips family constitution. That clause dictated that any creature that could potentially afflict the allergies of the family commonwealth, or which required unnecessary and taxing time requirements, must be deemed against the general welfare and thus *malum in prohibitum*.

I had five minutes to prepare my mental brief and make oral arguments.

I would not only learn responsibility from owning a dog, but I would act responsibly and play the role of a responsible dog owner. I would be relentless in my responsibility. Did I mention being responsible? I would love the dog, train the dog, and I would personally clean up its mess. Mom would never have to worry about it. Yes, if I could have my very own dog, that would be one thing Mom and Dad would never need to worry about! I would have a new middle name—Responsibility. The tin man needed a brain, the lion needed a heart, and Doug needed a dog. And what better dog than a pure-bred mutt with big brown eyes—one that had been abandoned by the world and providentially brought to me.

After an intensive cross-examination period by the Supreme Court, my dear mother handed down the ruling—the dog was mine.

Thus began my career as a home school attorney.

The Dogs of War

I named the pup Rusty and purposed to never forget the day that we met. More than thirty-five years later, it remains one of the most treasured memories of my childhood.

Rusty had so much energy. We used to play a game I called "war" in which I would chase Rusty and work her up into a frenzy, pretending to fight with her until she would growl and bark and yip with delight. War always ended with a happy belly-scratch—hers, not mine.

Our love affair continued. Rusty was a little thing, but boy, was she loyal. Especially when it really mattered.

In those days, we lived in a neighborhood populated by a gang of boys. They were the classic bullies—mean to animals, mean to children smaller than themselves—-just plain mean. One winter day I found myself face down in the snow after a showdown with the head bully—a boy three years my senior named Michael Steinkrause. The bully band circled the little conflagration and cheered Michael on. The dares and double dares were flying. He was hollering, and so was I. But he had thirty pounds on me, and I couldn't budge. Things were looking bad.

Just at the point when I was about to have my face rubbed in the snow, the attention of the crowd shifted. What at first was not easily distinguishable became increasingly clearer every second. There on the horizon appeared a missile with legs, traveling at shocking speeds and aimed at our little social gathering—it was Rusty.

At the sound of my voice in the midst of the commotion, Rusty had thrown her little body against her chain with such force that she broke free. She knew something bad was going down and was coming to do something about it.

The next thing I knew, that little dog had interposed herself between me and the face of Michael Steinkrouse. The more she growled and showed her canines, the less confident and more conciliatory Michael Steinkrause became.

I learned that day that a bully's bark is worse than his bite. Behind every bully is a coward waiting to be exposed.

From that day on, Rusty was not only my companion,

she was my newly appointed military *aide de campe*.

But there was a price to pay.

Several months later, the same bullies shot Rusty with a 22. rifle. God protected my dog, and she lived to play and bark and spend close to another decade with her master. In my mind, Rusty received a Purple Heart that day for being wounded in action. She was no longer just my friend and defender; she was a secret service agent who had taken a bullet for her master.

In the Dog House

There are at least four reasons why dads get dogs for their children. The first is that they want their children to experience what they did not. The second is that they want their children to experience what they did. The third is that they believe the dogs can contribute something helpful to the economy of the family—whether that is guarding the home, herding animals, or simply adding to the delight of family culture. The final reason is that fathers have compassion on the appeals of their children who dream of having their very own dog.

> *Just as a father has compassion on his children, so the LORD has compassion on those who fear Him.* —*Psalm 103:13, NAS*

In my case, it was a mixture of all of these motivations.

It was during our years in the Hill Country of Texas that we began to accumulate dogs. Two dogs in particular became "the dogs of our life." Their names were Yeller and Barkis.

Yeller was the quintessential family dog—a big, gentle, slobbery, patient yellow lab. She was and always remained the "momma" of our animal community.

In those days, we spent a lot of time at the animal shelter—maybe once a week. We liked to look at the animals, take them out, and play with them. Beall used these visits as a home school opportunity. The children learned about what to do and what not to do with animals; they learned about breeds; they became familiar with the personalities of different types of dogs and cats.

At the animal shelter we met Barkis. She was another "pure-bred" mutt—black with brown and a few white spots. Joshua named her after the main character from the book, *Barkis*, about a little lost mutt puppy. There was not a mean bone in our Barkis. She had a great personality and loved people. But we failed to fully train her out of her habit of wanting to lick everyone in sight, which sometimes scared little children. Barkis was the constant companion of Joshua and often followed him on his walks down the old country road to wait for Daddy.

One day another dog showed up—a very nervous, jittery Border Collie. The dog liked life on our Texas Hill Country property, so he stayed. Eventually, we named him Fly, after another famous sheepdog. We never really thought of him as our own dog, but more as a permanent guest.

Fly was one smart dog. But Fly appeared to have come from an abusive home. Whenever we placed a collar over his neck, he would roll over, cower, stick his legs in the air, and whimper. Once the collar was on, he would not stand up.

Candidly, I do not think much of psychology or psychological terminology, but Fly had such bizarre personality traits that he came to be known as the "poor psychopathic" pup. The most notable of these traits was his tendency to relieve himelf on pretty much everyone who came in contact with him. The more you tried to approach him, the more he cowered and relieved himself.

We had to move, and Fly had to go. But who would take him?

We placed ads in the newspaper and began to receive phone calls from would-be dog owners. The calls started coming in, but we had the same experience over and over again.

"I understand that you have a Border Collie that needs a home."

"Yes, Fly is a sweet dog with many admirable qualities, but in the interest of full disclosure, you should know that he relieves himself on whomever holds him."

Click.

After a dozen or so calls like this, we got a call from a man who specifically expressed an interest in owning a troubled Border Collie. We could not believe our ears. When he arrived at our home, he explained that he was a psychiatric nurse who understood all about this, so a cowering, bladder-challenged dog would be no problem.

Beall stood in amazement as the big nurse scooped up Fly in his arms.

"It's okay; I will take care of you," he told the dog.

We knew it was a match made in heaven. Off went Fly.

The Barnyard of Our Little Agrarian Fantasy

Like every good home school family, our dreams and aspirations eventually turned to experiments in agrarianism. The goal was not to become farmers, *per se*, but just to enjoy the healthy country lifestyle. Beall and I wanted to continue ministry and business in the city, yet raise our children in the world of Texas trees, happy cows, and grassy acres. In short, we wanted to have our cake and eat it, too.

For the first half-decade of our marriage, I worked for the Home School Legal Defense Association in the rolling valleys of Virginia. During our first two years, we lived in the horse capital of Virginia—Middleburg. We were broke, but the Lord blessed us with the ability to live on a beautiful and secluded fourteen-acre estate in exchange for caring for a retired racehorse and his companion pony. It was a grand lifestyle that even afforded us the opportunity to see the ladies and gentlemen from the Middleburg Hunt—on mounted horseback and wearing their brilliant red jackets—ride over the property chasing the elusive fox.

Later, we moved to Hamilton, Virginia, where we found an old home and affectionately dubbed it "The Cow House." The owner rented it to us for peanuts in exchange for our willingness to perform farm duties. At The Cow House we raised rabbits, played with two horses which we named Cyril and Emily, and cared for a herd of cattle. It was a wonderful homestead with many mysterious things to explore, including a big old barn built during the Second World War by Nazis who had been interred down the street in a prison camp. My boys and I spent lots of time in that barn exploring, transporting hay to the cows, telling stories, performing chores, and finding animal lairs.

Middleburg and The Cow House were both hearty and glorious experiences that convinced Beall and me of the benefits of country living. When we arrived in Texas, we hoped to continue and expand our dream, should God provide the resources for us to do so. Eventually this hope became a reality when we rented a large, unusual home on nine acres in the Texas Hill Country. The next step was to build our barnyard.

The Truth About Chickens

It started as a wonderful dream: We would have chickens—lots and lots of happy little chickens. And they would lay eggs—lots and lots of delicious eggs. And each morning my own dear little daughters would joyfully skip to the henhouse, wicker egg-basket in hand, and collect our breakfast.

That was the dream. Here was the reality.

The first few weeks after the building of our coop and the arrival of the roosters and hens was a time for fond memories. The little ones loved the chickens. They loved the morning ritual of gathering the eggs and then watching Momma cook them on the stove. Our dream was coming true.

One morning, my then three-year-old daughter, Jubilee, grabbed her wicker basket and headed to the chicken coop. True to her name, Jubilee has always been jubilant—a really enthusiastic, delightful daughter. Jubilee always sees the cup half full. She always thinks the best. Life is her oyster. And those little chickens were not only her personal friends, they were like her very own children.

But on this one particular morning, Jubilee's three-year-old world was about to be turned upside- down. She entered the chicken coop to discover a scene of carnage and mayhem.

The sweet little chickens of yesterday had become the bloodthirsty savages of today. In an apparent battle for hegemony of the coop, chicken factions had developed, the strongest of which decided the time had come to subjugate the weak. So they chased them, plucked all of the feathers from their collective chicken fannies, and left them to bleed and cluck in pain and agony.

Poor Jubilee was mortified. She came running and crying to her parents:

"Daddy, Mommy...the chickens...the chickens...the chickens are evil!"

Thus ended our jaunt with poultry.

But there was good news. This was the first time that Jubilee had ever seen pain and destruction with something she loved. She looked at everything with such pure delight. It had never entered her mind that animals might fight and kill each other. She was upset to the core. As hard as this was, however, it served as a great teaching opportunity for our daughter. It's a lesson we often share with our children:

"Once upon a time, there was no death or bloodshed. God made a perfect world in which animals like dinosaurs, chickens, bears, and lions all lived in harmony. They ate plants, not flesh. God described this world as "very good." But then Adam rebelled against God. Sin brought death. It brought eternal death. It brought physical death. Sin meant that animals would now eat other animals. It meant there would be pain. Every time you see something horrible, remember that it is always a consequence of sin, and there is only one remedy for sin—repenting of sins and believing in the Lord Jesus Christ. You sin. I sin. That means we need to run to Jesus and ask His forgiveness. We need to fall at his feet for He is our God and our Creator."

The Illegal Immigrants of the American Barnyard

Then there was the llama issue. We never owned llamas. We just visited neighbors who did. That was enough.

My experience with llamas taught me that there are three things one should never say to a llama. First, never discuss dental hygiene with a llama. Second, never call a llama "the illegal immigrant of the American barnyard." And finally, never, ever use the words "llama-burger" and "this may be your future if you don't start pulling your weight around here" in the same sentence.

You may console yourself all day that, after all, these are dumb brutes without the capacity of human speech. You may even remind yourself that God has made man to have dominion over the beasts. But should you be foolish enough to actually tell a llama to his face what you really think about him, remember this—God, in His providence, has equipped llamas with two qualities which, when matched with their violent tempers, rightly qualifies them as predatory animals.

The first is their ability to spit with an accuracy which would make an Olympic sharpshooter blush. The second is the capacity of the llama to manufacture oceans of noxious bile within the depths of their stomachs—no doubt stored near their dark hearts.

But should you succumb to temptation and disregard my above warnings by engaging a llama in dialogue, and should you value the company of family and friends, then please listen carefully to my counsel: The moment that diabolical creature lowers his ears—run! Run for your life. Run for the sake of generations yet to be born. Run and don't look back.

This leads me to the conclusion that if "chickens may be evil," llamas are more so.

Though chicken behavior has an appearance of evil, it is a junior varsity evil in comparison to the dastardly deeds of the malevolent llama. After all, it is one thing to send a sweet egg-collecting home school girl running to her daddy in tears after discovering that the hens of the coop have plucked the feathers out of the collective tuchases of their compatriots. But it is another thing altogether for a rabbit-eared, inedible pack-animal to lie in wait in order to launch missiles of expectoration on those who mean it no harm.

While chickens may be evil, it is clear to all who have eyes to see and ears to hear that llamas are monomaniacal, beady-eyed malcontents bent on spewing malodorous bile of the most pungent properties on those innocent passers-by who, out of nothing but sheer courtesy, stop to engage them in friendly conversation.

Just an opinion from somebody who "knows a guy" who had a very bad llama encounter in front of his family and friends. At least that's my story, and I'm sticking with it.

Penumbra and Emanation

This brings me to our two goats: "Penumbra and Emanation"—the two most elusive and law-breaking goats ever to grace the Hill Country of South Texas. Did I mention that they were extremely rebellious goats—and I emphasize "extremely."

Penumbra and Emanation—-strange names for goats? Not when you see goats as I see them: The first thing you need to know about goats is that they have only two missions in life. The first is to eat anything and everything in sight, and the second is to escape. These are their only goals in life. But my goats had an additional problem—they thought they were dogs. They wanted to hang out with the dogs, follow the dogs, eat the dog food, and generally act like dogs. More on that later.

And all of that has something to do with their names: The terms "penumbra and emanation" come from a famous United States Supreme Court case, *Griswold v. Connecticut*, which declared, for the first time, a Constitutional right to privacy. The context was a law concerning contraception. Finding no concrete Constitutional rule which would allow the Court to reach the conclusion they personally preferred, the Justices declared a "right to privacy" found in the "penumbras and emanations" of the Constitution. The Justices were saying, in effect, "This new rule may not be found in the black and white of the Constitution, but we like it, and we are sure that it can be found in the halo of ideas circling the document." In other words, when all else fails, make up law. It was a supreme act of judicial tyranny and rebellion. Since then, "penumbras and emanations" have been the source of every anti-family act of Constitutional legislation handed down by the Court. For conservative Constitutional attorneys like me, the phrase has become synonymous with a renegade judiciary that will not be bound by rules.

Back to my two goats.

Here is how the whole experience with goats began: Some years ago, I decided that the next logical step in our family experiment in agrarianism was the acquisition of goats. Knowing little about goats, but fancying the idea of our glorious flock of beasts happily bleating and following my children and me around our small, leased, country farm in the cactus-rich hills of Texas, I ordered my goats and waited with bated breath for their arrival.

Within sixty seconds of their disembarkment from the transport vehicle, they had escaped and were running wildly throughout the countryside, terrorizing the neighbors and wrecking yards.

My opinion of goats began to change.

Here is what I discovered in the weeks that followed: Goats are out-of-control maniacs that scream bloody murder when you approach them. They eat everything in sight, climb trees just long enough to pounce on your children, and delight in wreaking chaos, havoc, and devastation on the domestic bliss and otherwise peaceful dominion of the Christian country household.

What made matters worse was that our rebellious goats placed peer pressure on our dogs to misbehave. They would break free from the yard and coyly bleat at the dogs to follow them on a feeding and drinking frenzy through foreign lands.

We would remind Yeller, "If sinners entice thee, consent thou not," or even "bad company corrupts good morals." But despite our pleadings not to follow the example of our two rebellious teenage goats, Yeller's only response was to wag her tail and offer a big slobbery grin—in a yellow Labrador kind of a way.

The End of Penumbra and Emanation

Throughout all of this time, there was a nagging question which continued to bother me. If I am supposed to take dominion over an animal as intellectually challenged as a goat, what does it say about me that I can't do it? Doesn't the Bible expressly teach "for every kind of beasts, and of birds, and of serpents, and of things in the sea, is tamed, and hath been tamed of mankind" (James 3:7)? What about goats? And what about my goats in particular? After all, if a ninety-five-pound woman from Sea World can get a two-ton orca to flip in the air, then give her a kiss, surely I could teach these goats to stop climbing trees, thinking they are dogs, or leading the only real dogs I own into sinful temptation. Right?

That question was never answered. The day came when the Phillips family had to leave our happy experiment in agrarianism in exchange for a slightly more urban neighborhood where the residents did not take kindly to rebellious goats, bloodthirsty chickens, or spitting llamas.

As a going-away present from our family, we gave Penumbra and Emanation to a dear Christian lady from Mexico named Ana who lived in the Texas Hill Country and had become our friend. She did not speak a word of English, but we spoke a little Spanish. When we offered her the two goats, she seemed very happy. As best as we can tell, she let us know that she would take very good care of Penumbra and Emanation.

Just before we moved, we noticed Ana holding a big celebration for her friends. There was an open barbeque, much merriment, and an occasional comment about *buenas cabritas*.

We did not ask any questions.

Goose Quixote

The Phillipses have certainly had our fair share of run-ins with eccentric animals, but none was as loveable as a chivalric, but cantankerous, bird named Goose.

That was his name—Goose.

He was Goose the brave! Goose the persevering! Goose the indefatigable defender of the same country road where my little boy would walk and wait for the return of his father. We did not own Goose, but Goose was a daily part of our lives, and we felt that somehow he was a member of the family—a very cranky member of the family.

Goose lived near the entrance to our country street. He had a unique calling—to challenge every passing car to a duel. Goose was the Don Quixote of the feathered community.

You really had to admire Goose. Nothing intimidated him. No car was too big. No person too intimidating. If it was a car, it was fair game. If it was a stranger, look out! Goose had a job to do, and he was going to do it.

Every day we drove past Goose. Every day Goose blocked us from coming or going, honked at, charged our vehicle, and beat the front of the car with his beak. Not content to peck people, Goose would hurl himself at the car and peck the fender. Every day we dialogued with Goose, urging him to get out of the road. Sometimes we physically tried to move Goose, but Goose viewed that as a formal challenge. His response was to become more aggressive and peck us to the point where we inevitably retreated to the presumed safety of the car.

This went on for a long time. Hundreds of cars had a personal encounter with Goose. If geese were ever recognized for successful military operations against cars, Goose would have been an ace one hundred times over. He never failed to distract, annoy, and slow down cars. Most importantly, he never conceded the fundamental principle—when it came to that street, he was the boss! This was his town. It was Goose's domain.

In those days, our local church was meeting in our home—about 250 people on the Lord's Day. That translated to close to fifty cars on a Sunday, or one hundred opportunities (coming and going) for Goose to duel. I could just hear Sabbath visitors describing the experience: "I went to worship this Sunday, but all I remember is the crazy goose that tried to attack and kill me."

Goose's fame continued to grow. Children looked forward to seeing him. Cars drove extra slowly so as to do no harm.

Then one day it happened. Exactly how it happened remains a bit of a mystery to this day. Here is what we know: As Beall slowly drove her car past Goose's territory and up the country road, the old bird defiantly planted himself right in front of the two front tires of the moving vehicle. The next second, Goose was nowhere to be seen. Beall felt a thump, stopped the car, and backed up. There was Goose, lying in the road, wounded but not yet dead.

He looked at her, and she at him. Then Goose gave up the ghost.

My dear bride was inconsolable. At that time, Beall was close to five months pregnant carrying Honor. She ran to the home where the owner of Goose lived. Sobbing, she confessed to having "murdered" Goose. The neighbor looked at Beall and sympathetically replied, "Don't worry, he had it coming."

Beall was heartbroken. Goose was gone. How could this have happened? And what to say to the children?

Goose, poor Goose.

Our little children wondered—was Goose on a vacation from attacking us? When would he be back? Is he guarding other streets, attacking fresh cars now? Where is Goose? Similar questions began to come from our friends at church.

It took a while before Beall could talk about Goose. It was just too hard. The very thought of his defiant little waddle or his wild maniacal honk brought tears to the compassionate eyes of my wife. During that time, I ran interference with the children, but I could only hold off the questions for so long.

When the children learned of the death of Goose, they cried. But their tears were not so much for Goose as they were for their poor mother. Mom had been suffering thinking about how much the death of Goose would hurt her dear ones. That was a big revelation.

This is really the moral of the story: Children understand. They get it. Their hearts have the capacity for great compassion. Their simple, child-like faith allows them to receive and believe difficult realities.

Animal Mortality

Animal mortality has been a fairly constant theme in the Phillips household. The death of bugs, toads, and lizards has never made much of a dent. At least for our family, the connection between child and praying mantis is relatively non-emotional. But give an animal some hair, and all bets are off. There is just something about feathers and fur—what I call the "cuddly factor"—which contributes to accessibility of the animal and the sentimentality of my children. Over the years, we have had a steady flow of "cuddly" animal deaths. Big or small, when a cuddly animal dies, it is not easy.

Buddy the Hamster

Buddy was a hamster and beloved in the eyes of my daughters. He was one of the first of many hamsters that would eventually take over the Phillips household.

In our house, the hamsters have been kept in the girls' room and in our family room, both of which are locations where Vision Forum CDs are sometimes played. Now I am not saying that the hamsters understood the theology behind my recorded messages on the blessing of children and multigenerational thinking; I am simply pointing out that, once these creatures get babies on their minds, they don't know how to stop. Their commitment to prolific population was of such a scope that their total numbers exceeded fifty. Frankly, we stopped counting.

But before there was a nation of furry rodents living in my home, complete with official green cards provided by the Phillips girls, there was just Buddy and a few of his friends.

One day Buddy did something very inconsiderate. He chose to break the hearts of my dear ones by up and dying. After the first round of tears was shed, the girls made an important decision. Something had to be done. Buddy the hamster had been an admirable animal—a downright noble beast. Who would lament his death? Who would honor his memory? What ballads would be sung? Would future generations hear about Buddy the hamster?

Apart from decisive action, Buddy would be forgotten. But they had a plan. Several days later, preparations were complete for an elaborate goodbye for Buddy. Here is what happened:

The funeral cortage left the front of our home and slowly and mournfully traveled thirty yards from our door to the final resting place of Buddy.

A made-to-order coffin had been prepared. Buddy was carefully wrapped in a burial cloth and laid inside the hamster coffin. The children organized the procession that consisted of pallbearers (the brothers), mourners (two sisters), an officiant (Jubilee), and onlookers (everybody else). The participants were dressed for the occasion.

Ever so slowly, they made the lugubrious journey to the burial site under a big tree in the back yard. The mourners mourned. The onlookers looked on with compassion and interest. As to the pallbearers—any temptation to giggle was faithfully suppressed.

If anyone was waiting for someone to break out the trombones and play "When the Saints Go Marching In," they were waiting in vain. My girls knew nothing about Louisiana Jazz funerals. More importantly, they knew that Buddy did not have an eternal soul. He was an animal, and that means that when he died, he was gone forever.

Once they arrived at the gravesite, a formal pre-planned service began.

Jubilee began: "Dearly beloved, we are here to say goodbye to the most faithful hamster in the history of the world—Buddy."

The mourners sobbed.

The precise words spoken over the body of Buddy have been lost to the ravages of time, but I do know that they included more praises for the many virtues of Buddy the hamster, more tears from the mourners, and some vigorous exhortations to the onlookers to keep the memory of such a fine hamster alive for many generations. The event was capped with the singing of a solemn Christian hymn. At last, Buddy's cold, dead, furry rodent body was placed in the ground. The pallbearers filled in the hole with dirt and placed a rock on top to mark the site.

I wonder if there has ever been such an elaborate funeral for such a tiny furball?

There are two ways to look at the official farewell to Buddy. Some might cynically view it as an overly sentimental and distasteful homage to a critter. That is not how I see it.

Here is what I see: I see little girls who had been listening to their daddy and mommy talk for years about multigenerational faithfulness. I see them internalizing the concepts they were taught that multigenerational faithfulness involves proclaiming the great deeds of God in the lives of those who have gone before us. I see them taking that theme and applying it to the only significant loss within their family that they had experienced to date. In my view, the real message of the funeral of Buddy the hamster had less to do with a pet and more to do with young children showing a special type of honor to their parents, even as they hurt over the death of a friend.

Buddy was gone, but more hamsters would be born—

and then more, and more, and more. Eventually, time not only brought new hamsters, it brought new hamster deaths. But there were no more elaborate funerals and fewer and fewer broken hearts. The sheer number of hamsters and the increased responsibility of caring for them probably prevented the girls from developing the same type of attachments they had experienced during the early days. My little girls gained more maturity, and with that maturity, greater perspective.

But I knew the world had changed when, one day, a daughter announced to me, "Looks like some more hamsters have died this week, Dad."

"More hamsters? You mean your pets have been dying?"

Without blinking she said, "It's okay, Dad. You don't need to be sad for us. We know they are just hamsters."

Rascal A. Beak, R.I.P.

In the end, all pets die. But it is the untimely death of a truly great childhood comrade that creates a hole in the heart of a child that only time and perspective can remedy. The Lord sometimes uses these tragedies to season the hearts of boys and girls with compassion and to provide parents with rich insights about the preciousness of their little ones that the same parents might otherwise miss.

When the childhood love of an animal is tested by the death of that beloved pet, boys and girls often lack the vocabulary to express their feelings. It is the duty of fathers and mothers to compassionately help them process their experiences and articulate their emotions so that they can grow through the loss.

If the demise and burial of Buddy had been an endearing tribute to the death of a pet, the loss of Rascal A. Beak was one of the harder moments of my fatherhood.

When Joshua was about ten and Justice eight, they found a little grey bird by a tree in our yard. The bird was fluttering on the ground, apparently unable to fly away. Something was obviously wrong, so Joshua picked him up.

The first thing you need to realize is how the mind of a boy works. By the time a boy finds a lost bird and has concluded that it needs help, he has already named the bird, figured out a plan for teaching the bird tricks, and has designed in his mind an elaborate sketch for the castle he will build for the bird to live in. And it does not matter whether the bird is a blue jay or a chickadee; the winged wonder will become a pirate bird by learning to sit on the shoulder of the boy like "Captain Flint," the parrot belonging to Long John Silver from *Treasure Island*.

Our bird was a little baby pigeon, and Joshua and

Justice named it Rascal A. Beak. For the first week of Rascal A. Beak's captivity, he went everywhere with the boys. He lived in a little transportable wooden cage and learned to eat out of the hand of the boys. Their piratical aspirations were soon realized as well. Within a few days, they taught him to flutter to them and sit on their shoulders.

Perhaps in the future, Rascal A. Beak would have to be released to the world of birds, but at least for this season, he would sail the Seven Seas and conquer the wild, wild, West with the Phillips boys. For now, it was a dream come true.

But one day that dream came to an end. The boys were visiting their good friend Andrew. As usual, they had Rascal A. Beak with them. The purpose of the visit was to practice hunting, trapping, skinning squirrels, and making tomahawks—a typical day of adventure in the life of the Texas home school boy. But first, their mission was to build a castle for their bird. Rascal A. Beak would guard the castle while the boys hunted.

The castle, however, was built on sand, not a rock, and was unsteady. To the horror of my sons, the castle rocks came down upon the neck of the little bird. It was the end of Rascal A. Beak.

This was the first time that I saw my young son Joshua

so distraught that he could not talk very much for days. It just hurt too much. Justice was sad, but he hurt even more for his big brother who was not taking the death well.

The story ended with a burial. But not before Joshua drew a beautiful picture of his dear departed bird. On the picture, he wrote, "Rascal A. Beak, R.I.P." He showed me the picture and asked if neither the death of the bird, nor even the name Rascal A. Beak could be spoken of again in the Phillips household. That is when I really understood the pain my little boys were feeling.

My heart was filled with such compassion for my son. Even though my calling in life involves the use of words, no matter how hard I tried, I had no meaningful words to offer him. All I could do was hold him and tell him that I understood. He wanted to walk through this loss like a little man, and I wanted to be with him as he did.

It has been more than a half a decade now since the death of Rascal A. Beak. Today, Joshua and Justice are young men who gladly speak about the little bird and all their animals. They speak about the good times and the sad, about the victories and the failures. When it comes to animals, their season of "firsts" is quickly passing, but each of their adventures has added to their perspective on manhood.

Today, I looked at pictures of Justice, Joshua, and

Rascal A. Beak. Their faces were beaming with pure boyish joy as they played with the little bird. It reminded me of the preciousness of those halcyon days of boyhood and why it is important that fathers share these experiences with their sons. It reminded me that lost love hurts, but when it comes to animals—better to have loved and lost, then to have never loved.

Five years later, the picture of Rascal A. Beak is still an important part of my son's treasure chest.

Conclusion

Animals can be a delight or a distraction, but children are truly amazing. They are cute, adorable little sinners in need of redemption, but they are little sinners with qualities that Jesus identified as the key to eternal life.

> *Verily I say unto you, whosoever shall not receive the kingdom of God as a little child shall in no wise enter therein. —Luke 18:17*

The purity of their child-like faith gives them a capacity to believe great truths that "more enlightened" adults disdain. They hope in all things, trust all things, and think the best. They are quick to confess, ready to forgive, and willing to bare their hearts to others. They are also capable of a special child-like love so precious and unique that one rarely, if ever, sees it repeated in the world of adults.

God sometimes uses the care and love of animals by boys and girls to reveal these gifts of childhood to adults. When we see our children love deeply and with purity, we are reminded of a time when our own capacity to learn and love was unjaded by the cynicism of adulthood. When we see our sons and daughters truly delight in friendship with an animal, we are reminded of how much more important it is that we delight in our own children. God forbid that animals take precedence over humans or that animal love supercedes the intensity of relationships within the Christian family.

Thank God that He uses the humor of living with quirky animals to add color to the canvas of family life. Thank God that He uses the responsibilities of caring for the lives of God's creatures as a means of teaching stewardship. Most importantly, thank God that we can learn to know and love our children in unique ways that might otherwise be unlikely, but for the opportunity to see them love and lead animals.

In the end, it may be that God uses the experiences our sons and daughters have with animals to school the parents even more than the children.

> *A righteous man regardeth the life of his beast.*
> *—Proverbs 12:10*

CHAPTER 5

THE MAN'S LIBRARY
How Wise Fathers Use Books
to Disciple Future Generations

The cloak that I left at Troas with Carpus, when thou comest, bring with thee, and the books, but especially the parchments. —2 Timothy 4:13

My father has never been a wealthy man by the financial standards of the world, but he gave me many rich treasures: He gave me life. He gave me an education to which he contributed substantially through personal discipleship. He gave me his hard-earned good name. He gave me a love for the Word of God and a child-like acceptance of the truth of that Word. He gave me many challenging, inspiring, and wonderful experiences that helped to define my view of manhood.

And my father gave me one physical possession that intersected with each of the above—he gave me a library, a library that he built over many decades, and which was hand selected by my father for me.

But it all began when my father taught me the joy of reading and the blessing of being a son in his father's library.

As a boy, my father's library was always a thing of awe and beauty. I loved the rich mahogany-stained shelves of the sacred inner sanctuary called "Dad's Study," but more importantly, I viewed the old square room as a time vault into the unfolding history of my father. The shelves of the library were not only thick with books, but phenomenal artifacts from Dad's world travels. The books themselves came in every shape and size, with dust jackets and without, in multi-volume collections, and as single volumes—but the vast majority were quality hardbacks. The various seasons of my father's life—from his childhood at the Boston Latin School, to his undergraduate work at Harvard, to his various epochs of service on behalf of Christ and country—seemed to be chronicled for every family member to see through the many books which he had acquired over a lifetime of adventure, experience, and intensive reading.

Often, the information contained in the pages of these books was less important to me than the story of what these books represented to my father at the time he purchased them. I found clues handwritten in the margins; clues which pointed to priorities, challenges, struggles, epiphanies, and victories which he may have experienced at the time that the books were first opened and read by him. In some cases, as with his copy of R.J. Rushdoony's *Institutes of Biblical Law*, a flip to the back cover revealed notations of the date when he completed the first, second, and even third reading of the same valued book.

The mere presence of my father's library taught me to respect and love important books. And it increased my respect for my father as a man. My father had chosen not to invest his limited and precious resources in sports paraphernalia or entertainment, but in documents, literature, and resources that filled our home with knowledge. In my father's library, I met and grew to love the men that my father respected. There were shelves dedicated to the writings of the great Alexander Solzhenitsyn, to the life and legacy of George Washington, and to great reformers and heroes of Christianity. In my father's library, I met Shakespeare, Tacitus, and Blackstone. They were all there, and I knew that if they were important to my father, they needed to be important to me.

I watched him rise early in the morning and read. For many years my father's daily reading regimen included close to a half-dozen newspapers, journals, books, and, of course, the Bible. This took place early in the morning in his library and sometimes lasted two hours or more. Dad would sit in his great leather chair, with piles of magazines and newspapers around him, and unopened cartons of books—fresh arrivals from the various book clubs to which he belonged—accumulating on the floor and tables beside him.

Many of those books were designated for his children—and their future libraries. Dad was always thinking ahead. He was committed to sending us out someday with substantial libraries of our own. The Phillips children rarely received toys on birthdays and holidays— we were given books, and lots of them. And more than a few of these volumes were rather ambitious in substance and content—like giving me college-level texts on *The History of the Greek City States*, or Xenophon's *Persian Expedition* when I was still in grade school. I may not have read Xenophon as an eight-year-old, but I eventually got around to most of these books. By the time I left my father's home to begin the process of establishing my own household, those many years during which Dad invested in his son's future library had created a sizeable literary nest-egg. Thanks to Dad, I was able to bring thousands of substantial books into my marriage—many of them signed and dated by my father.

The library my father began building for me when I was only six continues to grow as he adds to it year after year. For my fortieth birthday, I received a gift box with forty individually wrapped books on subjects as diverse as economics, theology, and foreign policy, each book hand selected for the occasion by my father.

What Makes a Great Library?

Knowing I lov'd my books, he furnish'd me,
From mine own library with volumes that
I prize above my dukedom.
—*Shakespeare,* The Tempest

The greatest men I have known have had great libraries. They love their libraries because it is there that they go to consult with their mentors. The noted evangelist and preacher, Samuel Davies, put it this way: "The venerable dead are waiting in my library to entertain me and relieve me from the nonsense of surviving mortals."

To this day, when visiting a friend's home, I love to

be invited to look at his library. I can tell so much about the man by looking at the books he has collected, how he prioritizes them, and whether they are unopened museum pieces, or well-worn, dog-eared tools of dominion.

But libraries don't have to be massive to be significant. A great library may be a carefully selected library, a wisely organized library, or a library that simply accomplishes a specific purpose of its designer. Some great libraries are gloriously cluttered and filled with mysterious treasures to be rediscovered. Others are meticulously organized. Still others are a combination of the two. But one thing all great libraries have in common is old books. The books must be old, because most things worth reading were written prior to the advent of the twentieth century, and many of the best things to read are out of print, which means nothing but an original edition will do. There are many exceptions to this rule, but it is fair to say that most men who appreciate the importance of building a man's library want to stock it with old books.

Then, of course, there is the issue of aesthetics. Even if certain old books came back into print, the aesthetic of reading an old edition remains one of the allures of the man's library. It is not just the superior bindings, paper, and design of pre-twentieth century books, but the sensation of holding a literary artifact that was likely handled and read by men from other centuries. It is the look of the book, the thickness of the paper, and the very smell of the document that makes an old book so attractive to those men who aspire to build a man's library for the future generations.

Whether the books are old or new, the man's library should be dominated by well-bound hardbacks as these are the only books that will stand the test of time. These books should be cared for and well preserved, but at the end of the day, books are not objects of worship; they are tools. They should be handled, read, and shared with others. Since great books and important libraries should be passed from one generation to the next, I favor men writing in the margins of their books. Many of the Founding Fathers did the same, and for good reason. Marking a book personalizes it and allows the reader to leave a memorial of his thoughts at the time, as well as a reference guide from which he can draw ideas for teaching, writing, or speaking. History records that both the sons of several notable Founders, as well as future generations of Americans, were able to benefit from the fact that the more ancient fathers left clues to their true, unpublished thoughts through the penciled commentary found in the margins of the volumes which lined their shelves.

In Search of the Man's Library

The love of learning, the sequestered nooks,
And all the sweet serenity of books.
—Henry Wadsworth Longfellow

My two favorite "man libraries" were both created by national leaders to honor their fathers. The first is the King George III library, presently housed in the British Museum in London. Stunning in its beauty and scope, this is the type of library that most of us will only dream of. One part ultra-rare antiquities and another part beautifully-preserved first editions, the King George III library may be the closest thing we will get to a modern-day equivalent of the lost library of Alexandria. Spacious, warm, and accessible, this one-room library was built to preserve and present the great works of the past and present world. On one shelf, you can find Joseph Story's *Commentaries on the Constitution of the United States of America*, and on another, beautiful editions of Chaucer, Milton, and Bunyan. On a third, one can find actual stone-carved documents from the reign of Nebuchadnezzar, and on a fourth, original carvings of laws from the days of Sargon II.

The second library is found in Quincy, Massachusetts.

As a physical expression of appreciation for the literary legacy of one generation for the next, few family libraries compare with the one built by Charles Francis Adams for his father, John Quincy Adams, the Sixth President of the United States. The President left a clause in his will requesting that his son build the library. Charles Francis not only honored his father by following his father's directions and specifications for a physical library building, but he also honored the intent of his father by using the library to write important books. In fact, he trained his sons, Brooks and Henry, to do the same, the latter of whom finished his famous nine-volume *History of the United States* in the Adams library built by his father. Explaining the importance of the library to him, Brooks Adams would comment, "I need a sitting room where I can entertain my friends, but I must have a library where my books can entertain me."

Neither John Adams nor John Quincy ever entered the library that would be dubbed the Stone Library, but their pictures are on the wall, and numerous artifacts from their lives remind everyone who enters of the importance of the great patriarchs and their continuing influence on the generations that followed.

Still open to the public, the Adams family library is home to more than 14,000 volumes and is remarkable for its simplicity, its depth, and the multigenerational vision it communicates. The message of the library is simple: The best educations are taught from father to son. Important tools of such an education are the carefully selected books which are handed down from one generation to the next. It is the duty of sons to preserve the intellectual legacies of their fathers.

The library screams generational thinking! One is reminded of John Adams' observations once shared in a letter to his wife, Abigail:

> *I must study politics and war that my sons may have liberty to study mathematics and philosophy. My sons ought to study mathematics and philosophy, geography, natural history, naval architecture, navigation, commerce, and agriculture, in order to give their children a right to study painting, poetry, music, architecture, statuary, tapestry, and porcelain.*

The structure of the Adams family library is a simple rectangular building, about thirty by thirty feet, with true Puritan New England simplicity. Having said this, the beauty of the floor tiling, the richness of the shelving, and the magnificence of a room in which every square inch has been designed with purpose, leaves the visitor breathless. Of course, the statues and paintings which visually chronicle the life of the Adams family and their friends is impressive, but it is the leather-bound books that captivate and enthrall one's attention—thousands of them, most ancient first editions that tell the story of the education, the passions, and the vision of one of the most influential families in history.

Building Your Library

In 2004, I visited the Adams library with my father, my sons, and my good friend, author and antiquarian, Dan Ford.

We entered the room and just stood with our mouths gaping until I finally broke the silence.

"This is a man's library," says I.

"Yes, and it even smells like a man's library," another chimes in.

To which Dan replies, "Ah, the smell! There should be a cologne called 'Old Books.' I would wear it every day."

A few minutes later one of our team exclaims, "Wow, I would love to have a man's library like this."

"Be careful, the Tenth Commandment forbids us from coveting our neighbor's goods," another responds.

At which point my dad ended this line of the dialogue by retorting, "Gentlemen, I don't covet this library; I just want one exactly like it."

Dad was joking, of course, but there was a point behind it—it is right and good that men should desire to leave a legacy of wisdom for their children—and the written word is a key means of accomplishing that goal. For this reason, the Christian man's library should be a reflection of the core principle that "the fear of the Lord is the beginning of wisdom" (Psalm 111:10).

Because the Bible is the only perfect book that instructs man in the pursuit of knowledge and wisdom, a Christian man's library is built with the recognition that even the best books are merely supplemental to the Holy Scriptures. But wisely selected supplemental books are an invaluable asset to the Christian man; an encouragement and an incentive to dive deeper in search of the pearls of God's written revelation. That is why I favor building libraries around histories, biographies, literature, and research tools which allow the Christian man to better understand the person and character of God, the universe He has created, and His providential hand in history.

With a little bit of thought and research, any Christian father can start the process of building a Christian man's library. To begin, one must understand that a great man's library is not a museum, but a toolshed of knowledge, a scientific laboratory of learning, and an office for self-improvement.

Wise fathers invest in their children. That investment involves enormous amounts of time dedicated to discipline, prayer, discipleship, and training. It is good to leave a financial inheritance to faithful sons, but it is better to leave a legacy of wisdom. By leaving a carefully built library for your sons and daughters, a man can hope to do just this. Because the purpose of knowledge and wisdom is not intellectual satisfaction, but preparation for a life of spiritual warfare and dominion works for the Lord. The Christian man's library may be an inviting, treasure-laden sanctuary of peace, but its mission is preparation for combat readiness. It is a classroom for Christian manhood.

Through my father's example, I came to believe that, in some ways, a man's library is a reflection of the life of the man: The library tells you what the man has been thinking about and what ideas he prioritizes. It is filled with the icons and artifacts of a man's life. But like the man himself, a thoughtful library takes a lifetime to build.

In the case of Charles Francis Adams, the family library took forty years to build. The first thirty-nine years were spent collecting, collating, and organizing the books and papers of the Adams family. The actual construction of the fireproof building took much less time. In his diary of September 28, 1870, Charles Francis Adams writes:

"The Library may be pronounced complete today. It was cleaned and the last mechanic left it at five o'clock. It has taken about six months to construct a single room. Now the labor of removing the books will begin. . . ."

The apostle Paul thought it important enough to remind Timothy to "bring the books." Wise fathers of the twenty-first century would be well-advised to do the same. The sooner fathers get about the business of collecting and reading important books, the sooner they can invite their sons to join them in that special cove of repose known as the man's library.

CHAPTER 6

THE LEAGUE OF GRATEFUL SONS

*How Generational Honor
Preserves Nations*

In the last sixty years, fewer people have visited the island of Iwo Jima than have climbed Mt. Everest. Resting at the base of the Bonin Island chain, Iwo is one of the most remote and isolated clumps of volcanic rock and sand in the Pacific. Except for vegetation and the small Japanese military installation that guards the lonely airport, there is little sign of life anywhere on this remote four-and-a-half mile long outpost.

Of all the remaining battlefield monuments to the Second World War, Iwo Jima is singular. It is an entire island largely untouched for sixty years and dedicated to the memory of one month in the Spring of 1945 when more than 100,000 men were locked in a battle unprecedented for its bloodshed and iconic in its significance to the American people.

Even beneath the surface there are reminders. More than eleven miles of underground tunnels and fifteen hundred rooms once housing 21,000 Japanese defenders remain. One can still find bayonets, boots, and even skeletal remains in open view, undisturbed and exactly where they have rested for more than half a century— haunting reminders to a vicious conflict in which 70,000 American fighting men descended on this speck of an island for what would become the defining battle in Marine Corps history.

This is a destination where old men go to remember the fallen comrades of their youth. It is an island where sons go to honor their fathers.

One day a year, the Japanese government opens Iwo Jima to the small handfuls of veterans and their families and friends who come to remember and pay homage to the fallen.

The Faith of Our Fathers film team covered over twenty thousand miles during a span of three weeks during our journey of honor.

On March 12, 2005, the Vision Forum Faith of Our Fathers film team hit the beaches of Iwo Jima with more than eighty aged veterans who battled on those same black sands in 1945. Our day on Iwo was part of a journey of honor—a three-week tour of the Pacific in which we sought to record on film the wisdom of those surviving men whose lives were forever marked by thirty-six days of hellish warfare. It was a mission of multigenerational faithfulness dedicated to honoring our fathers and remembering the providence of God over the World War II generation.

Though we were astonished by the stamina and persevering spirit of these grandfather heroes, we knew they would never again return to the island. There will be no seventieth celebration with ninety-five-year-old men walking the beaches, combing through the caves, or climbing the 546-foot Mt. Suribachi. This was it—the closing adieu to an event which has remained with these men every day of their life for sixty years. This was the last time to speak of ancient battles with ancient warriors. It was the last time to smell the air, to sift the sand, and to weep where beloved brothers exchanged with blood their own futures so that children yet born could have the hope of peace. It was the final farewell.

But among our group of pilgrims was a very special band of brothers, each united by a common loss, a common legacy, and a common heart of gratitude. Theirs was a story within the broader story; a record of devotion so compelling that we often labored late into the night to capture, record, and process each precious testimony.

We called them "The League of Grateful Sons"—and their story is the true tale of boys who spent their lives loving and dreaming about the fathers who never came home from Iwo Jima.

The Father Who Never Died

February 18, 1945

Dear Johnny Boy:

Tomorrow morning Dad is going to play war with all his strength, so that Mommy can sing to you "A Wee Little Lad" and mean every word of it.

Red will be right along side Dad. You would laugh to see the way we are dressed. I am carrying so many guns, and they are sticking out on all sides.

As the man of the house, Dad is counting on you to continue in helping Mom in every way.

When I come home, I will have many stories to tell you about those ships and planes and jeeps and trucks.

Thanks for praying for Dad.

Your Proud Dad

"Johnny Boy" was five years old when he received this letter from his daddy—Lt. Col. John Augustus Butler, Sr. It was the latest of many communications his father had sent since departing for the Pacific. Each note was filled with encouragement, manly counsel, and fatherly love prepared from fields of battle by a man who would not allow a world war to interfere with his duties to instruct his son.

But this letter was different. It was the last communication "Johnny Boy" ever received from his "proud dad."

Note the date—February 18, 1945, the eve of D-Day. On February 19, Lt. Col. John Butler would hit the black sands of Iwo Jima as commander of 1st Battalion, 27th Regiment, 5th Marine Division, leading over one thousand men into the fight for their lives against an entrenched Japanese enemy. Fourteen days later, the popular battalion commander and devoted father of four would lose his life in the performance of his duty, fighting on the frontlines.

It is now sixty years later, and "Johnny Boy" is a grandfather.

I first met John Butler, Jr. on the plane to Guam and was immediately taken by this sixty-five-year-old son's irrepressible passion for his father. Within moments of making his acquaintance, he was unfolding documents and showing me precious letters of the man he loved.

He literally grabbed one member of my team, looked him in the eye, and asked, "Have you heard of my father? Do you know the things he did?" He pulled out an accordion file-folder, crammed full of dozens upon dozens of letters—letters exchanged between "Johnny Boy" and "Daddy"; love letters written between his father and mother; letters written to his mother by men who served under his father's command.

And then there were pictures—scores of them— photos that catalogued his father's life and testimony.

Great things happen when fathers love and disciple their sons. That is why, for sixty years, this son has loved the daddy who never came home. For sixty years, he has read and re-read his father's instructions to him. For sixty years, he has remained devoted in his heart to the man whose wisdom and love, communicated through battlefield letters, has been a guiding light in his life.

He put it simply: "I feel like my father has always been here with me."

At this point, the words of the Eternal Son came to our minds:

> *Then answered Jesus and said unto them, 'Verily, verily, I say unto you, The Son can do nothing of himself, but what he seeth the Father do: for what things soever he doeth, these also doeth the Son likewise. For the Father loveth the Son, and sheweth him all things that himself doeth' —John 5:19-20*

The Heroism of the Fathers is the Legacy of the Sons

> *I will open my mouth in a parable: I will utter dark sayings of old: Which we have heard and known, and our fathers have told us. We will not hide them from their children, shewing to the generation to come the praises of the LORD, and his strength, and his wonderful works that he hath done. For he established a testimony in Jacob, and appointed a law in Israel, which he commanded our fathers, that they should make them known to their children: That the generation to come might know them, even the children which should be born; who should arise and declare them to their children: That they might set their hope in God, and not forget the works of God, but keep his commandments. —Psalm 78:2-7*

My first meeting with "Johnny Boy" took place on the journey to our base camp in Guam.

For the sixtieth anniversary of their father's death, John Butler, Jr. and his younger brother Clinton (only four months old when his father was killed) decided to return to the island where their father was ushered into eternity. It was to be a pilgrimage of sonship to remember and give thanks for the man who in death left a legacy of love and devotion.

It gives a son confidence to know his father was a man of character. John, Jr. describes his father this way:

My father's story is one of love, the love between him and my mother, love for and faith in God, a love for humanity and the men he led, and great pride in the Marine Corps he served. Those whom he led and those who knew him, speak of his exceptional character, genuine friendliness, and the superb leadership of his battalion in training and in combat.

In the providence of God, several of the men traveling with us knew the devoted father of John, Jr. and Clinton. They had served alongside Lt. Col. John Butler during the war and were able to give first-hand accounts to his sons.

Most notable among these men was Col. Gerald Russell, the senior ranking veteran of Iwo Jima on our trip. A member of the first U.S. Marine Corp Officer Candidate's class in American history, and a battalion commander at the age of twenty-six, Russell (now eighty-eight) was wounded on Iwo the day Lt. Col. Butler was killed. Russell, who following Butler's death would later take command of his battalion, explained:

> *There were a lot of leaders men followed who they did not like. John Butler was not among them. He was a man's man. Everybody loved him. He was the kind of man that would prepare his boys for battle by going man to man, putting his arms on them, and whispering personal words of encouragement to them.*

Growing up, "Johnny Boy" knew this about his father. His mother told him. He heard report after report from men who had been friends with his dad. But he also knew it experientially. He knew it because John Butler, Sr. was a man who modeled true fatherhood by taking time to prioritize the mission of giving counsel to a son—even in the thick of battle.

John, Jr. explained how his father's life of heroic leadership at home and in the battlefield became an enduring testimony of hope in his own life:

His image and deeds always loomed large and have been a major influence in my own life... His smiling image was always on the mantelpiece over the fire place in the living room of our family home, and my mother, who never remarried, and never considered another man in her life, spoke often of their life together in stories told over and over again.

John Butler, Jr. spent many hours opening his heart with the Faith of Our Fathers film team. As he presented to us ancient letters, we knew we were peering into something sacred and wonderful. His father had written him directions on how to live life. These directions were a guidepost for him. His father had demonstrated tender love through his written words. These words were the vehicles whereby the boyish hurt over the loss of a father was transformed into a lifetime of honor, gratitude, and vision. In short, his father had given him an inheritance more valuable than gold; he had given himself.

In addition to his general call for his son to be a boy of faith and prayers, two themes emerged in the Butler letters: (1) Some things are worth fighting for; and (2) Take care of women and children.

Some Things are Worth Fighting For

October 21, 1944

Dear Johnny Boy:

Don't worry, Johnny Boy, your daddy will find his way home again. It will be a long time because there are many things to do. I have to go to a land where little boys your age don't have friends named Eddie and Connie, nor can they play the whole day through, for they have no Mamas and Papas, as you and Eddie have, but instead they belong to a thing called a state and a wizened old man they call their emperor and god. I have got to help restore them to their Mamas and Papas; and, Johnny Boy, one day you will be doing the same thing, for many of us have learned to bend our knees without bending our hearts.

Daddy

"Johnny Boy" learned that some things are worth fighting for. There is a time when a man must leave the comfort of his home and give his all in defense of family and freedom. Evil exists, and when that which a man most cherishes is in peril, he must not cower and run. He must face the enemy head-on.

This father made it clear to his son that he was fighting

for a way of life—he was fighting to preserve the sanctity of his home, to ensure the safety of his wife, and to secure hope for his children. He was fighting to protect his family from tyranny and his native land from those who would set themselves up as God.

John Butler's letters to "Johnny Boy" were a call to bold manhood. In them, John, Sr. communicated truths on leadership and faithfulness. His letters to his son conveyed, in unmistakable terms, that the men fighting on Iwo were fighting to secure a future for their loved ones. They were fighting for the opportunity for their sons to one day lead as men and embrace the principles they stood for—to act with honor, purity, and courage in establishing families of their own.

Women and Children First!

January 26, 1945

Dear Johnny Boy:

Mommy tells me in her letters that you are growing to be quite a man. You understand, Johnny, don't you, that while Daddy is gone you must take good care of Mommy, Mary Joe, Morey, Lola, and the new baby. All men must know how to dress by themselves, how to be gentlemanly and kind all the time. You must help Mommy by helping around the house and by helping watch Monty and Clinton.

A big kiss for you,

Dad

One of the most remarkable messages of the John Butler letters is that men must treat women properly. This was the principle of the Butler patriarch, both on the battlefield and the homestead. John Butler, Jr. explained to us how his dad's intense chivalry fostered an "uncommon love affair" between his mother and father that lasted a lifetime.

"My mother was a beautiful woman, but she never remarried," John explained to me. "She remained forever devoted to the memory of my father and the task of raising her sons."

"Johnny Boy" was raised to believe that the strong must sacrifice for the weak. Men must be willing to give their lives to protect women and children because "greater love hath no man than this: that a man lay down his life" for those he loves (John 15:13).

John, Jr. removed from his father's sacred archive yet another letter—a testimony to a father who, while caught in the throes of the Second World War, took time to admonish his son in the ancient chivalric code.

February 6, 1945

Dear Johnny Boy:
Johnny, always remember that as long as Dad is away, you are the "man of the house," and you must protect Mommy, Lola, your sister, and little brothers.

Lovingly,

Daddy

Iwo Jima Was a Battle of Men for Women and Children

We live in an effeminate society where politicians and pastors have ignored the age-old principle of male sacrifice taught to us by Christ in the Gospel of John. All too often, they have sold their manhood cheap for a mess of pragmatic porridge they hope will lend them the title of "culturally relevant" or "politically effective." This is particularly clear on the issue of women in the military. As the number of girls and mothers returning from foreign wars in body bags rises, our collective consciousness towards the moral wrong of placing our nation's daughters in harm's way becomes increasingly seared. Like the murder of the unborn, we have learned to be tolerant of that which is barbaric and unnatural. We have even learned to cheer when women go off to war to die in the place of men.

But it was not so on February 19, 1945. Iwo Jima was a battle fought by men in defense of women and children. When I asked the combat veterans of Iwo what they think it would have been like to have nineteen-year-old girls hit the black sand beaches with them, they stared at me and stammered, usually unable to process my question. The thought was incomprehensible.

There were no female combatants on Iwo Jima. There were not even female non-combatants. Quite simply, there were no women. Of the more than 100,000 Japanese and Americans fighting over that rock in the Pacific, not one was a woman. This was a battle for men.

The message of "women and children first" was not lost to the fathers on Iwo Jima. Their letters tell the stories of dads who made it their mission to communicate the ancient chivalric code of manly virtues to their sons by example and by written word.

Sixty years later, their sons have not forgotten. John

Butler, Jr. remembers. He remembers because the code of his father was written down. It has been preserved for more than half a century, during which time it has been repeatedly read.

"We are Here to Honor Our Fathers"

Leonard Scott Isacks, Jr. (41) and Fletcher Bryan Isacks (38) stood on the shores of Iwo Jima on March 12, 2005 in honor of 1st Lt. Leonard Smith Isacks, Jr. their fallen grandfather. Leonard and Fletcher Isacks are precisely the type of men who our team had hoped to meet. Big, strong, hearty, confident, outspoken—they approached me after I delivered a brief address to the Iwo veterans by announcing to me, "We are making this trip to honor our father and preserve the legacy of our grandfather."

But that was not the half of it.

Over the course of our adventure in the Pacific, my staff came to know and appreciate these grateful sons for their devotion to multigenerational faithfulness. Where other men have hobbies, the Isacks brothers have devoted significant energies to recording, preserving, and studying the more than twelve hundred pages of letters documenting the lives of their father and grandfather, men they describe as having a deep, abiding Christian faith.

Now they returned to honor their grandfather who died during the bloody battle, and to fulfill their father's life-long dream to visit the island—a dream which, due to his untimely death three years ago, was never realized.

Like "Johnny Boy" Butler, the Isacks brothers carried with them cases of documents that reveal the Christian faith, manly leadership, and fatherly devotion of their ancestor. In 1943, their grandfather, Leonard Smith Isacks, Sr.—then father to three children—joined the United States Marine Corps. On February 19, 1945, 1st Lt. Isacks hit the beaches of Iwo Jima as operations officer for the 5th Motor Transport Battalion, 5th Marine Division. On D+1, 1st Lt. Isacks was mortally wounded in his foxhole. The following day, he died aboard the hospital ship *S.S. Samaritan* and was buried at sea.

Incredibly, during his twenty-three months of service in the Marine Corps leading up to his death, Leonard and his wife, Sue, wrote more than twelve hundred pages of letters to each other, each of which have been preserved.

I found one of 1st Lt. Isacks' letters especially poignant. On Sunday, December 17, 1944, he gave his sons the following bit of counsel they would cherish and re-read throughout their lives:

December 17, 1944

My dear little boys:
Above all, my boys have courage, have courage to do the things
that you know are right. Never be afraid to fight for what you
think is right. To do those things you need a strong body and a
brave heart; never run away from someone you may be afraid
of; if you do, you will feel ashamed of yourself and before
long you will find it easy to run away from the things that you
should stand up and fight against.

God Bless You,

Daddy

Bryan and Leonard (uncle and father to the two brothers we met) were ages eight and five, respectively, at the time of their father's death, yet they hung tenaciously to the testimony of their departed dad. Their lives were defined by his example.

Following in his father's footsteps, Leonard Scott Isacks, Sr. joined the Marine Corps in the late '50s where he served with distinction. He would later receive the Navy Marine Corps medal for heroism for saving the life of a fellow Marine. Leonard left the Marine Corps a Sergeant to start his family and raise his two sons, Leonard

Scott Isacks, Jr. and Fletcher Bryan Isacks—our traveling companions, and two impressive members of the League of Grateful Sons.

Our Fathers Have Told Us, Therefore We Have Hope

We have heard with our ears, O God, our fathers have told us, what work thou didst in their days, in the times of old. How thou didst drive out the heathen with thy hand, and plantedst them; how thou didst afflict the people, and cast them out. For they got not the land in possession by their own sword, neither did their own arm save them: but thy right hand, and thine arm, and the light of thy countenance, because thou hadst a favour unto them… [W]e have not forgotten thee, neither have we dealt falsely in thy covenant. Our heart is not turned back, neither have our steps declined from thy way. —Psalm 44:1-3,17-18

The clear message of Holy Scripture is this: Fathers will teach the next generation, or they will lose the next generation. Fathers will speak to the next generation about the many providences of God in protecting and preserving them, or the next generation will be without hope. Fathers will cultivate gratitude, or they will produce a generation of ingrates. God will not be mocked: We will either walk beside our sons and teach them to honor their fathers, or there will be no nation for America to defend.

There is another side of the story of the League of Grateful Sons which I reluctantly relate. It is the story of tragic fathers and lost children. We met some of these men, too—men in the twilight of their lives who still remain aloof and uninvolved with their children and grandchildren, unwilling to speak of the past, and uninterested in offering counsel for the future. Theirs was the tragic legacy of hopelessness, and it showed.

The bottom line is this: Sons must ask, and fathers must tell. This is the most ancient principle of generational faithfulness. It is a father's job to communicate to his sons verbally and in writing. He must communicate a code of conduct. This code must include the many virtues of manhood including devotion to the God of the Bible, fair fighting, purity, the defense of women and children, and gratitude for the country which God has given to us.

Leonard Smith Isacks, Jr. and John Butler, Sr. did just this. They did this at home and from the battlefield. Their sons and grandsons have drawn strength from their enduring written testimony—and do so even today, over sixty years later.

Will All the Daddies Come Home?

The truth is this: Despite lives cut off in their prime, fathers like John Butler, Sr. and Leonard Isacks, Jr. did more to communicate hope and meaning to their sons than do typical fathers who enjoy a lifetime of opportunity. Through the simple acts of letter-writing, fatherly counsel, and manly leadership, these fathers of Iwo Jima made a deposit of counsel and wisdom into the accounts of the sons' lives which yielded unimaginably rich dividends to the present day. Their words continue to inspire. The principle of the patriarch has become the heart of the sons.

One of Leonard Smith Isacks' final letters to his boys beautifully models this principle:

December 17, 1944

My Dear Little Boys:
I won't be able to give you a Christmas present personally this year, but I do want you to know that I think of you all of the time and feel very proud of the way you have been helping your Mother while I am gone. I know that it is natural for young, healthy and strong boys like you are to want to play and have fun all of the time; but I do want you to think about helping Mummie, because it is so hard for her to do everything while I am gone.

I know that you would like to give me an X-mas present too, so I will tell you what you can do, and this will be your X-mas present to me. Everyday ask Mummie if there are any errands that you can go on for her, and when there are errands to run for her say "sure Mummie" and give her a big smile; then during the day go up to your room and look around, if there are toys scattered all around, or you left some of your clothes on the floor; pick them up; also, when Mummie is busy trying to clean up the house, don't leave her by herself, but ask Mummie if you can help take care of baby sister. If you will do these things for me, that will be the finest X-mas present that you could give me. Oh, yes, and CC, are you eating your meals like a real man now?

Well my boys, I guess you often wonder why people fight and have wars, and why lots of daddies have to be away at X-mas time fighting, when it would be much nicer to be at home. That's a hard question to answer. But, you see, some countries like Japan and Germany, have people living in them, just like some people you and I know. Those people want to tell everyone what they can do and what they can't do. No one likes to be told how to live their life. I know that you certainly wouldn't like it if one of the boys in the neighborhood tried to tell you what church you should go to, what school you should go to and particularly if that boy was always trying to "beat up" some smaller and weaker boy. You wouldn't like it, would you? And, unfortunately the only way to make a person stop these sorts of things, or a country like Japan or Germany, is to fight them and beat them . . . and teach them that being a bully (because after all that's what they are) is not the way to live and that we won't put up with it. What does all of this mean to you? Just simply this, my boys, Dad, doesn't want you to ever be a bully, I want you to always fight against anyone who tries to be one; I want you to always help the smaller fellow, or the little boy who may not be as strong as you; I want you to always share what you have with the other fellow. . . . If you and lots of other boys try to do things that Dad has been talking about in this letter, if may be that people will not have to fight wars in the years to come and then all of the Daddies of the world will be home for Christmas, and that is where they belong. Perhaps some of the things that I have been talking about . . . you don't quite understand. If you don't, Mummie will explain them to you, as she knows. . . .

God Bless you, Daddy

Leonard Smith Isacks, Jr. was one daddy who never did come home. But through his devoted fatherhood expressed in thousands of pages of letters filled with faith, exhortations to manly virtues, and tenderhearted compassion, he secured a permanent residence in the heart of generations yet to be born—generations who would remember him as a patriot and patriarch whose legacy of love shaped the life and destiny of a grateful family dynasty.

Sixty years later, his children's children's children speak of him, look at his pictures, study his words, and vow never, ever to forget. They are yet another testimony to the eternal truth that God blesses sons who honor their fathers, and honors fathers who bless their sons.

These are the true children of Iwo Jima—an army devoted to the memory of their fallen fathers. They are the latest inductees in a six thousand-year society of father-honoring boys known as "The League of Grateful Sons."

> *Remember the days of old, consider the years of many generations. Ask your father and he will show you; the elders and they will tell you. —Deuteronomy 32:7*

CHAPTER 7

THE COMING OF
MAHERSHALALHASHBAZ

Towards Epistemologically
Self-Conscious Baby Names

Moreover the Lord said to me, "Take a large scroll, and write on it with a man's pen concerning Maher-Shalal-Hash-Baz. And I will take for Myself faithful witnesses to record, Uriah the priest and Zechariah the son of Jeberechiah." Then I went to the prophetess, and she conceived and bore a son. Then the Lord said to me, "Call his name Maher-Shalal-Hash-Baz; for before the child shall have knowledge to cry 'My father' and 'My mother,' the riches of Damascus and the spoil of Samaria will be taken away before the king of Assyria." —Isaiah 8:1-4

Welcoming Baby

It is four o'clock in the morning, and I am going room by room through the house waking my children. My first stop is the little boys' room, then the girls' room, and finally the big boys' room. In each room I approach my sleeping child, put a hand on their shoulder, and whisper one sentence in their ears.

"She's here."

I see a yawn, then a stretch. Sleepy eyes begin to open. Little arms reach for my neck, and I hear a whispery, "Hi Daddy."

"She's here."

It is right about this moment that the explosion takes place. One by one, off come the covers, and up bolt the children. Then, with cheetah-like speed, each pounces on the ground, leaps for the door, and flies down the hallway to Mommy and Daddy's room.

But they don't go in.

They don't go in because Daddy has a rule that everybody has to line up together outside the door. They have to wait for Mommy to give Daddy the sign that she is ready.

The children are beaming with smiles, and jumping up and down. The smaller ones are still rubbing sleep out of their eyes, but the others are bright-eyed and bushy-tailed, squealing with anticipation. The excitement is palpable.

Then I have the privilege of saying something that I will only be able to say a few times in the course of my life:

"Children, meet your new baby sister."

It is at this point that the doors to our master bedroom fly open to reveal their beautiful mother sitting up in her bed with a baby in her arms. There are "oohs" and "aahs", kisses and hugs.

Six of our eight children were born at home with the help of faithful midwives, and six times we have enjoyed the privilege of welcoming our children to the room where, just two hours beforehand, their mother was in labor.

For the next hour, each child will hold the baby in his arms for the very first time. My daughters especially have the "itching arms syndrome"—where a little girl stretches out arms that simply cannot be satisfied until they are filled with a warm bundle of life. But each child waits his turn.

We talk. We laugh. We snuggle on the bed. We analyze every feature of the newborn baby. And we introduce our baby to being part of a large family by spending the first few hours of its life all together on the big bed in Mommy and Daddy's room.

It is one of the most unforgettable and happiest moments in our lives.

But there is an unspoken question that must always be answered. It is on everybody's mind at this moment, even as it has been for nine months:

What is the name of this precious new child?

Our Story

This is the story of how the Phillips family names our children—not only how, but why we believe that the name that a parent gives a child is one of the most important duties of parenthood.

At the time of the publication of this book, Beall and I have eight children on this Earth: Virginia, Providence, Honor, Faith, Jubilee, Liberty, Justice, and Joshua. Each child is as precious as the other to us. The Lord took one of our babies into eternity. His name was Victory, and though we never held him in our arms, his memory is precious to us as well.

As Christian parents who desire a legacy of generational faithfulness, so many of our hopes and dreams are directly connected to the future of our children. And we have given each of them names that reflect this fact. Each name was bathed in prayer. Each name was studied and subject to much deliberation.

We are advocates for "epistemologically self-conscious" baby names. That is a high-falutin' way of saying that, in our household, we want the very process of naming our children and the names themselves to reflect the theology, the worldview, and the priorities of the Phillips family.

Over the years, both the names of our children, as well as the size of the family the Lord has given to us, have generated many wonderful conversations. Both have sparked delight, curiosity, and emulation from some, and occasional disapproval from others.

I want to tell you our story, but first, please permit me to begin with a little perspective on "the name game."

The Name Game

What's in a name? Maybe more than you realize.

Your parents give you many things, but one of the most important is your name. You begin and end your life with it. It is the one moniker that you carry with you all the time, wherever you go. It never leaves you.

In fact, the gift of your name is so significant that, long

after you are dead and buried, your name will continue to be used by others when they are talking about you. If you happen to be a famous person like Noah or Alexander the Great, that could mean thousands of years.

At the beginning of your life, your name is a form of identification, a term of endearment, and sometimes a window into the priorities of your parents at the time of your birth. As you mature, so does the value and meaning of your name. As people get to know you better, your name becomes more than simply a word for identification, but the verbal personification of what you are as a man or a woman. This is why "a good name is more valuable than great riches." It is why one of the most precious inheritances a parent can leave for his children is a good name. By the end of your life, your name has become synonymous with who you are, or at least what others perceive about your life work and your character.

Your name is likely to become one of the most widely used proper nouns in your vocabulary and the vocabulary of those close to you. Over the course of your lifetime, you will probably hear someone call you by your name between two and four million times, depending on factors like where you live, your profession, your involvement in church and community, and the number of people in your family. So get used to it.

And that is just the amount of times you will hear yourself addressed by name. This does not include the potential tens of millions of times that others will use your name to talk or write about you when you are not with them.

Some names appear better suited for certain individuals than do others, but in a universe ruled by the sovereign God of the Scripture, we can be assured that no name is ever given to an individual which does not carry with it some providential implications for that person's life.

Naming Children in Twenty-First-Century America

In twenty-first-century America, there are many factors which influence a parent's decision about what to name their child, including personal preferences, whim, and status. There is even a trend for some parents to select names that provide a perceived competitive edge in the professional world.

There are parents who check Social Security number data to avoid names that are overly trendy. *The Wall Street Journal* reported that some parents living in a market-driven society and feeling intense pressure to give their children names that will help them in the work force actually hire professional baby-naming consultants to help them to "brand" their children. These consultants employ mathematical formulas and data search engines to determine whether or not a particular name has positive or negative associations. These experts also evaluate names based on their ethnic origins, phonetic elements, and popularity.

Sometimes the difference between true vision, on the one hand, and genuine foolishness, on the other, is clearly a matter of perspective or divergent worldview. In other cases, foolishness should be pretty self-evident. Consider the 2008 example of a New Zealand couple who lost temporary custody of their nine-year-old daughter for naming her "Talula Does The Hula From Hawaii." The naming of his son and daughter Dweezil and Moon Unit, respectively, by celebrity rock musician Frank Zappa never raised custodial issues, but certainly caused the general public to scratch their heads.

Marketing strategies? Competitive edge? Obvious foolishness? Does any of this make sense to the Christian parent?

I don't think so. But neither does it make sense to me that parents should pick a name based purely on whim. John is a fine name, and so is Mary, but giving them to a child for no reason other than that you can't think of another name will do little to inspire your child in the future. Both excellent names are rich in meaning, history, and profound biblical significance. How much better to name a child for one of these reasons?

My thesis is this: The naming of a child is one of the most important decisions you will make on behalf of your son or daughter, so be deliberate. Make an "epistemologically self-conscious" choice. Be biblical. Consider your reasons and motivation for the name. Make sure they are consistent with Scripture. Be prepared to carefully articulate your reasons to others.

Consider also the message this name is sending to your child and the world with which he or she will spend the rest of their life interacting. When picking names, it is fine to consider sound, meter, popularity, ethnic background, meaning, association, and family history, but, in the final analysis, you should use his name to motivate your child and encourage him to persevere before the Lord. This means selecting names with the understanding that the day will come when you are prepared to give a meaningful, biblical explanation for the name of your child.

Family Revival and the Naming of Children

We are told in the press that traditional Bible names are losing favor within the broader culture. But this demographic is not true in homeschool circles. The same revival that is turning the hearts of parents to their children is turning parents back to the Scriptures where they find names that inspire and motivate.

For many years, I liked to introduce a bit of humor into the middle of my speeches at homeschool conventions, especially when I was speaking to an audience of three thousand or more.

At a strategic moment in my speech, I would stop and say:

"Excuse me, but is there a Joshua in the audience? Joshua, I have a message for you. Joshua, would you please raise your hand?"

Inevitably a sea of hands would wave.

Everyone would laugh because they understood the point I was trying to make.

Beginning in the 1980s, it seemed that most families in the homeschool movement had one son named Joshua. Joshua is not only the name of a book of the Bible and of one of the greatest Bible heroes, but it has an inspirational meaning—"The Salvation of Jehovah."

The same could be said of other important Bible names. Home educators were responsible for significantly contributing to a revival of meaningful Bible names. These parents were sacrificing to build multigenerational legacies. For many parents, giving children Bible names and virtue names became a reflection of their vision of victory for their families. Their hearts had turned toward their children. They aspired to see their children be mighty warriors for Christ. Consequently, they would give their children names based on scriptural virtues or names that point to the heroes of history from the Bible. Because their theology reflected an appreciation for both books of the Bible, they would often draw from the rich treasure trove of names found in the Old Testament.

I think a strong historical argument can be made that the resurgence of parents giving important virtue names and Bible names to their children often follows spiritual revival. A classic example is the Mayflower Pilgrims, one of the godliest groups in Church history.

Four centuries ago, a spiritual revival took place in the little congregation pastored by a man named John Robinson and made up of families who would one day lay the cornerstone of religious and political freedom in the United States. The Pilgrims signed their Scrooby Church Covenant in 1606. It was the height of the Puritan

Reformation and approximately the same time that we can observe a marked change in the way that parents named their children. Instead of popular names like "Mary" and "John," parents began to select virtue names like "Remember," "Resolved," "Wrestling," "Love," "Desire," "Fear," "Patience," and "Humility." They chose these names as a reflection of their commitment to Christ, and many of the names have become an inspiration to modern Christian parents.

Of course, the greatest case for "epistemologically self-conscious names" comes from the Bible itself. The Scripture reveals that the names of children are very important to Him. God even modeled the importance of names, by giving names to his creation. He called the light "day". The name Adam is related to the Hebrew noun "ha adamah" which has been transliterated "ruddy" or "man of red earth" which appears to be a declaration of unique supernatural creation by the Lord and a reminder that man is but dust and will someday return to it (Genesis 3:19).

Names were very important to Adam. As the first man, he became the world's first taxonomist, naming all the beasts of the field and fowl of the air. But perhaps the most important name Adam ever gave was to his wife. The Bible tells us exactly the intention behind the name

Eve: "And Adam named his wife Eve because she was the mother of all living" (Genesis 3:20).

Most of the names of the great patriarchs carry rich spiritual and prophetic significance. Enoch means "dedicated." Abraham means "father of many nations." There are hundreds of examples. One way to translate Methuselah is essentially "after this, judgment." He died in the year of the Flood. (How would you like to live 960 years with everyone greeting you, "How are you doing, 'After this the Judgment'?" For one thing, people knew that as long as he was alive, they were safe.) In the Scripture, we see names that are descriptive of the circumstances of individuals. We see names that praise the Lord. And we see historic names repeated through generational lines, perhaps to bless the new child with a name reflective of the best qualities of an heroic ancestor.

Meaninglessness and the Naming of Children

The sad truth is that most children don't know the meaning of their names. They assume that their parents named them on a whim. Often these children are right. Their parents rarely, if ever, speak to them about their names precisely because the parents themselves see little meaning in the names. Perhaps they did name them based on nothing more than a whim.

The real message here is meaninglessness, and the children of our modern world are sinking in a sea of it. Meaninglessness is the theme of modern education, modern entertainment, and the modern business world. For most children, the only meaning they experience is living for the moment. But how could we expect otherwise when their parents look at life through such a lens?

Life is very different for the Christian. In a Christian universe, everything has meaning. Everything is meaningful because we live in a world created by Jesus Christ, held together by the power of His Word, and filled with eternal purpose. It is Christ Himself who is the central principle of interpretation for everything in this universe—including the naming of children.

How Names Take on a Life of Their Own

Names play such an important role in the life of a child that they can actually influence that child's behavior. This is especially true when parents emphasize the significance of the name and draw appreciative connections between the character and interests of the child, and the meaning of their name.

I have a daughter named Jubilee. She is supremely

jubilant and has a passion for understanding Christ. Justice is a man who cares deeply about what is right and what is wrong. Joshua's middle name is Titus which means "a man who walks with giants." He has a pure-hearted faith and loves to be around wise, older men. My son Honor is a very tender-hearted son who is especially concerned about honoring his parents. My wife's name is Beall, a family surname deeply rooted in early American history and dating back to the late seventeenth century when her ancestor, Ninian Beall, was a member of the Prince George's County House of Burgesses in Maryland.

In the Phillips household, Beall and I love to speak to our children about their names. I want each child to know that everything about their life has great meaning, their name included.

One way we remind them about their names is through the use of a family catechism. The family catechism is a series of questions and answers that remind our children about the priorities of the family, important facts to remember about our family history, and biblical worldview commitments that we embrace. The Phillips family catechism is in a state of constant development, but the present Question #33 reads:

> **Question:** *What is the significance of the name "Liberty"?*
> **Answer:** *First, it is a reminder that where the Spirit of the Lord is, there is liberty. Second, it is a testimony to the liberty of Christ in the lives of your parents at the time of Liberty's birth. Third, it is an acknowledgement of our family's gratitude for the providence of God in America.*

I have written this question and answer for her, because I want her to love her name and to know that her Mommy and Daddy love her name. By memorizing the answer to our family catechism question, Liberty will always have a concise explanation of the reasons why her parents gave her such a special name. More importantly, she will know that her name was so rich in meaning and so precious to her parents that they required her to know that meaning, and they spoke of it with joy in their hearts every week of her life.

How My Father Used My Name to Encourage and Inspire Me

My father named me Douglas Winston after two of his heroes—Douglas MacArthur and Winston Churchill. Both MacArthur and Churchill were men who demonstrated unflinching courage and singular leadership at one of the darkest moments of the twentieth century. But for both men, Western civilization might look quite different today.

From my earliest days, my father spoke of these two men. He often drew the link between my name and my namesakes. The essential message I got was this: "These were great men who led nations, now you go and do the same thing, Son."

But it did not stop there. My father filled my library with books about my namesakes. He read their biographies at the dinner table. When we traveled the country by car, he often played books on tape that helped me to understand MacArthur and Churchill better. Dad brought me to historic locations where those men had distinguished themselves as courageous men. He took me to Fulton, Missouri, where Churchill had given his famous "Iron Curtain" speech, and to Norfolk, Virginia, where I spent the day with Mrs. Douglas MacArthur, the widow of the five-star General.

Talking about my name and my father's heroes was a constant reminder of my father's worldview, of his priorities, of his love for me, and of the potential he saw in my future. I think it is fair to say that my father began grooming me for leadership the moment he gave me my name.

It is a wonderful thing for a father to believe in his

son and to use the icons of that boy's life—his name, his education, his heroes—to motivate him. When a son feels the confidence of his Christian father's love and sees meaning in his life, it inspires the boy to believe that "I can do all things through Christ who strengthens me."

Everybody Gets Into The Act

"Daddy, did you pick the name I thought of for the new baby?"

"Not telling!"

"Oh please, Daddy. Tell, do tell!"

"Not telling."

"Can't we please name the baby 'Moose'? I like 'Moose'."

"It's not at the top of the list, Sweetheart."

"Just a little hint?"

"Not telling."

"I know, I know...if it's a girl, it's going to be..."

"Not telling."

"Oh please, Daddy. P-l-e-a-s-e!?"

"Don't worry, Dears. My little *shayneh kepelehs* will be the first to know."

Naming our babies is a family affair. Everybody gets into the act. Although the final top-secret decision is left for Mom and Dad, the whole family is involved in the naming process.

Boy, do the opinions fly.

Some of the most colorful ideas have come from our children. Joshua was convinced that the baby that would someday be Jubilee should be named "Moose." Liberty disagreed. Her formal vote was for "Squanto." And when Faith was about to be born, Liberty petitioned for "Flower."

Names like "Moose", "Squanto", or "Flower" are usually round one for the little children. They are sort of "ice breakers" in a long process that may last months. During this time, we talk with our children about the biblical principles for naming children as we understand those principles. We remind each child about the reasons why we gave them their names, and we urge everyone to stand unified as a family in prayer as we seek the face of the Lord on such an important decision.

Names come at different times. Sometime the name is clear to us before the birth of the child. Other times we don't settle on the name until we can actually look at the baby, hold him in our arms, and pray for him. In the end, Mommy and Daddy will make the final decision, but the children will be the first to know.

The second on the list to learn the name of the

baby is usually Mom and Dad. It is the process of telling grandparents the names of their grandchildren that has generated some of the more humorous moments in our family life.

The Coming of Mahershalalhashbaz

At some point in their marriage, many Christian couples have what I call a "whopper moment" with their extended family. This is the time when you call your parents to tell them about an important decision you have made which you know is probably not going to make sense to them. In fact, they are probably going to think you are crazy. For some couples, this whopper moment happens when they announce a decision to home school their children.

The scene has been repeated thousands of times. It goes something like this:

"Mom and Dad, we believe the Lord is leading us to teach our children at home."

"You mean that you are not going to give my grandchildren a real school education?"

"Not exactly. We *are* going to be educating our children, we are just going to be doing it at home."

"Why would God want you to deprive your children of a real education?"

"Mom and Dad, we believe we can give the children a better and godlier education than the school system."

"What about socialization?"

These whopper moments are part of life. You have them, and your parents probably had them when you were a child. They are actually healthy because, if handled properly, they help to bring maturity to the family, to establish legitimate jurisdictional boundaries, and can even be used as an opportunity to demonstrate great respect and honor in the midst of possible family differences.

In the Phillips family, home schooling was never an issue with our extended family. From the beginning, we always received exceptional support and encouragement. In the case of my own parents, they not only accepted it, they actively practiced it themselves.

Now it is one thing to home school your children, but it is another to give them atypical names like Liberty, Justice, Jubilee, and Providence. In fairness, these names have never caused a lick of fundamental concern, but they have been the source of great wonderment and speculation whenever a new baby arrives on the scene. The raging question is always—what will Doug and Beall name the baby? Will there be a whopper moment at the birth of the next child?

With such a buildup of expectation, I hate to

disappoint. So I concocted a plan and got the children in on the plot. Within hours after the birth of our sixth child, I was on the phone with my parents. Here is a paraphrase of the conversation:

"Praise the Lord, Mom! I have great news. God has given you a new grandson."

With cool reserve my mother asks, "And what did you name the child, Doug?"

"Well, I'll get to that in a moment, Mom, but boy are you going to love it."

"So, what did you name the child, Doug?"

My children are squealing with delight.

"Well, Mom, let me give you some good news about the name first."

"Good news?"

"It's a Bible name—and not just any Bible name."

Silence.

"In fact, it was a name God specifically picked out for the son of Isaiah."

More silence.

"Oh, and wait till I tell you the meaning of the name. It's just fantastic!"

More silence.

"Okay, here goes...In Hebrew, the name means: 'To speed to the spoil, he hasteneth the prey.' Isn't that great?"

I think I hear a gasp on the other end of the phone.

"Wait, Mom, there is more. It only gets better," I tried to assure her. "You are going to love this name. Really.... In fact, it's the very longest name in the entire Bible."

I hear a thump on the other end of the phone, as if somebody has fainted, or a glass has dropped to the ground, but the sound of heavy breathing reassures me that my beloved mother is still there.

"Okay...here goes....Mom, I am pleased to introduce you to your newest grandson: Mahershalalhashbaz Phillips!

And she believed me.

Meanwhile, the Phillips children are writhing on the floor.

"Poor Mimi. Poor Mimi...Tell her, Daddy...Tell her the real name...Please, Daddy."

In the end, I confessed the fib, and we all shared a good laugh. The real name of our baby was Howard Honor Phillips—Howard after my beloved father, and Honor after the principle of the Fifth Commandment. The boy would be known as "Honor." Praise the Lord.

After the possibility of Mahershalalhashbaz, Howard Honor Phillips seemed like a downright respectable name.

One translation of the name "Howard" is "brave-hearted, guardian of the home..." And from the moment he was born, Howard Honor Phillips looked like his illustrious grandfather, the former candidate for President of the United States, and a man whose life has been distinguished as a brave-hearted defender of the unborn. Another dream had been fulfilled. God allowed me to name my child after the most influential man in my life—My father.

Payback

Five years after the Mahershalalhashbaz incident, I found myself standing before an audience of just under two thousand people at the closing night ceremonies of the San Antonio Independent Christian Film Festival. Less than twenty-four hours earlier, I was at home helping to deliver my eighth child—a beautiful baby girl.

But, I was not standing alone. To the delight of friends and family (and the possible shock of some in attendance), my amazingly hearty wife was standing there with me, newborn baby in her arms. Beall had told me she felt great and wanted to come personally to introduce our baby to the world. I agreed.

The camera focused on Beall and the baby as a live

image of mother and child was broadcast to all those in attendance. I joyfully introduced our new child to the world, but said nothing about her name.

What was the name of the baby? Many wondered.

But there seated in the front row of the Lila Cockrell Auditorium that night was my very own father—and new grandfather, Howard Phillips. Not one to miss an opportunity for some well-deserved payback, my father proceeded to announce to those inquiring minds—"The name of the baby? Didn't you hear? Doug and Beall named her Sabbath Leviticus Phillips, of course."

And they believed him!

CHAPTER 8

THE WAR ON FATHERHOOD

Why We Must Choose Between Patriarchy and Patricide

Patricide is the act of killing our fathers. It can take many forms. Dishonor can be a form of patricide. To dishonor a father is to strike at one of the defining relationships in the universe—that of the Father and the Son. Revisionist history is a form of patricide. When historians attack the spiritual forefathers of a nation, or when they pervert the legacies of the past, they engage in a form of cultural patricide. But whether the act of patricide takes the form of physical murder, a dishonoring rejection of authority, or historical revisionism, the result is always the same—to cut off the future from the past and to ensure the destruction of the individual and the community.

The very first prophecy in the Scripture (Genesis 3:15) concerns Satan's attempt to destroy the godly seed. Because Christ-centered family unity and multigenerational continuity are so central to the perpetuation of the Church, we should not be surprised that a primary focus of Satan's work has been to sever the relationship between fathers and sons.

This principle was graphically illustrated to me fifteen years ago during a visit to sub-Saharan Africa. At that time, my father and I were working with the victims of terrorism when we met Endabo Musa. As a young man, Musa was taken from his African tribal village and brought to Patrice Lumumba University in Moscow during the heyday of Soviet African expansionism. His father, the local tribal chief, had released him with the expectation that he would be receiving a world-class education. In point of fact, he and hundreds of others like him were taken from their parents to be indoctrinated and trained in the arts of terrorism. The Soviets' goal was to indoctrinate these boys, many of them sons of local leaders, return them to Africa, and then destabilize the region.

Now here is the point of my story: With tears in his eyes, Musa explained to us that one of the first orders of business for a Soviet-trained African terrorist was to go back and kill his own father, thus breaking with the past, showing true allegiance to the new Soviet philosophies, and ending the history of multigenerational continuity which had existed in the tribes for hundreds, if not thousands, of years. Thankfully, the story has a happy ending. In his case, Musa was sent to kill not only his father, but also a Christian preacher. Heavily armed and accompanied by other terrorists, Musa entered a packed soccer stadium where the preacher was delivering a message. Before he could perform the wicked act, the words of the preacher touched the heart of Musa who abandoned his mission and became a Christian. Last I heard, he is a pastor living in Germany.

The Soviets had brilliantly adopted the old Satanic strategy—get the boys to forget their fathers, to reject their fathers, and even to kill their fathers, and you capture the nation.

The biblical response to patricide is patriarchy. Patriarchy presupposes that fathers are to be honored. They are to be recognized as sacrificial leaders; as the chosen vessels of God for protecting, providing for the family, and instilling vision. Patriarchy presupposes that it is not just a father's role to teach his children to succeed, but to succeed him. Patriarchy is inherently life-oriented.

It is honor-directed. Of course, there are perversions of patriarchy with which we would have nothing to do, but biblical patriarchy is central to the long-term success of any nation because at its core is the idea of Christ-centered, multigenerational faithfulness.

Absentee Fathers vs. Visionary Patriarchs

One of the contributing factors to the spirit of patricide in America today is the fact that so few modern fathers take the time to build truly meaningful relationships with their children.

Boys are crying out for a relationship with their fathers, but fathers are too consumed with other priorities until the situation with their sons reaches crisis level. Modern fathers have come to accept as normative the idea that the sum of their involvement in the life of a boy is attendance at a few athletic events and the occasional chat. Some surveys indicate that, on average, the American father spends a maximum of six minutes a day with his son. The absence of fathers in the life of their sons, coupled with the relegation of spiritual matters to the domain of womanhood, have rendered us a nation populated by fatherless families. And a nation of fatherless families is a dying nation. Perhaps this phenomenon is why the Bible, in the very last verse of the Old Testament, links true revival to the turning of the hearts of fathers to their sons.

Our colonial forefathers understood the importance of fatherhood. In his book, *Obedient Sons: The Discourse of Youth and Generations in American Culture, 1630-1860* (University of Massachusetts Press), Glenn Wallach documents the fact that the Puritan pulpit was regularly populated by preachers who emphasized father and son discipleship and multigenerational vision. Many of these preachers had themselves come from a long line of faithful patriarchs. A personal favorite is the great Puritan preacher Cotton Mather, son of the Rev. Increase Mather, a member of one of the most godly and influential families in American history. Like his father before him, Cotton was a scholar and devout student of Scripture. His father's emphasis on covenant succession and multigenerational faithfulness inspired Cotton to become an ultra-prolific author (more than 450 books), a scientist (who introduced the smallpox vaccine), and a herald to the sons of his generation to honor their fathers. As historian George Grant has reminded us, it was George Washington himself who described Mather as "undoubtably the Spiritual Father of America's Founding Fathers."

When asked the reason for his many accomplishments and abilities, Cotton explained, "I was simply the fruit of a well-watered tree." In 1715 he addressed the New England legislature with the following words:

> *One generation should make way for another. . . Let them in the generation that is passing off, be willing to pass. Let them in the generation that is coming, be willing to be likewise passing. . . . Oh Children, Beware of Degenerating from the godliness of your Ancestors. . . . Ah, New England, we fear, we fear, there is apace fulfilling on thee that Word. . . . there arose another generation after them which knew not the Lord.*

A Presidential Lesson in Discipleship

These words were not lost on the people of the day. Less than a century after Mather warned the people of New England to embrace multigenerational faithfulness, a very famous, very busy man was separated for a season from his son. This man had grown up in the land of the American Puritans. His own father had been a great man who had taken time to disciple him, as had been done by fathers in their family for generations. Zealous not to allow distance to diminish his fatherly duties, he penned the following words:

> *I advise you, my son, in whatever you read, and most of all in reading the Bible, to remember that it is for the purpose of*

making you wiser and more virtuous. I have myself, for many years, made it a practice to read through the Bible once every year. I have always endeavored to read it with the same spirit and temper of mind, which I now recommend to you: that is, with the intention and desire that it may contribute to my advancement in wisdom and virtue. My desire is indeed very imperfectly successful; for, like you, and like the Apostle Paul, "I find a law in my members, warring against the laws of my mind." But as I know that it is my nature to be imperfect, so I know that it is my duty to aim at perfection; and feeling and deploring my own frailties, I can only pray Almighty God, for the aid of his Spirit to strengthen my good desires, and to subdue my propensities to evil; for it is from him, that every good and every perfect gift descends. My custom is to read four or five chapters every morning, immediately after rising from my bed. It employs about an hour of my time, and seems to me the most suitable manner of beginning the day.

The author was President John Quincy Adams. A man of profound integrity, Adams understood the responsibilities of fatherhood. Though Adams did receive superior formal education, his character, his vision, and his worldview were largely shaped by his own father, President John Adams, who gave his son not only personal instruction, but opportunities while still a youth to venture into the world of men, ideas, and action. Consequently, we see John Quincy, at the ripe old age of fourteen, officially serving his country in the Court of France. Remarkable!

I was so impressed by John Quincy's commitment to Christian fatherhood that I took his letters and published them in a book entitled *The Bible Lessons of John Quincy Adams for His Son*. From my perspective, this book is important, not for the substance of the theology presented (the Adams family theology had been in decline for several decades), but because it is a record of a very busy man who did not allow his public responsibilities to detract from his fatherly obligations.

I must honestly admit that, even among the greatest proponents of biblical orthodoxy today, there are precious few who as eloquently and passionately communicate a love for Holy Scripture to their children as did John Quincy Adams. There are fewer still who would take the time to write seven thoughtful letters to a son, exhorting him to be a student of Scripture.

Fatherhood and the "P" Word

For many years now, I have been deeply impressed with the importance of fatherhood, family, vision, multigenerational faithfulness, and covenant succession. I believe that God means these concepts to be defining in the life of a Christian

THE WAR ON FATHERHOOD

man. These are not mere words, but living, breathing realities that constitute key themes in biblical history. These concepts are best summarized in a much maligned, but biblically significant word—patriarchy. Taken from the Greek *patria* (father) and *arche* (beginning), it embodies the idea of man as a father, leader, prophet, protector, provider, resident historian, vision-communicator, and covenant-keeper for the family.

Patriarchy presupposes a passion for children. The promise from God to Abraham that He would multiply this man's progeny and make them mighty on the Earth was a defining motivation in Abraham's life. Historically, men of God have craved children—lots of them. The more the better. Children were perceived as a source of blessing, a source of wealth, and a tool for advancing the Kingdom of God. The Bible even describes them as the Godly man's "reward" (see Psalms 127 and 128). Of course, it has not always been God's will to send children. Sometimes he closes the womb. God always knows what is best, and His plans are not to be resented or despised. The point is, however, that historically it was unthinkable for a Hebrew or Christian father to actively try to prevent the blessings of God or to cut off his reward.

Recognizing that, from the beginning, Satan wanted to destroy the godly seed, my wife and I entered marriage with the vision that we would actively seek the Lord for as many "arrows" as He would send, though we specifically desired twelve. Our prayers were answered early in our marriage with the birth of two sons (Joshua and Justice), followed by three daughters (Liberty, Jubilee, and Faith Evangeline), then two more sons (Honor and Providence), Victory, whom the Lord took, and the adorable Virginia Hope.

The Patriarch

In 1994, I was a young husband and father traveling on a train to meet my wife, when, moved with awe for the significance of the gift of family, I penned the following words as a vision statement and dedicated it to my wife. The poem is a special reminder to me of my covenant vows with my wife and the glorious privilege of fatherhood. I encourage you to read it at the dinner table during your family devotions:

> *More noble than the valiant deeds of shining knights of yore,*
> *More powerful than earthly plights that make the rich man poor,*
> *More kingly than a royal throne or a lion with his pride,*
> *Is he whose babes sleep well at night sure Daddy will provide.*
>
> *There is a sprit in this land, and Jezebel's her name.*
> *She's calling you to leave your home for power, fun, and fame.*

She wants your wife, your children too—she'll never compromise,
Until your house is torn in two by listening to her lies.

But though a hundred thousand, million men may fall prey to her lures,
And wives en masse *leave home in search of "more fulfilling" chores,*
Though preachers praise, and friends embrace, her pagan plan of death,
Stand strong and "quit you like a man" with every blessed breath.

Stand strong and rise, O man of God, to meet this noble call;
The battle is not, new you see; it's been here since the Fall.

Your wife is your helpmeet, my friend, and not another man's—
So care for her and keep her far from Mistress Jezi's plans.
Protect, provide, and give to her your undivided life,
This is the dear one of your youth, your precious bride, your wife.

And rally to those tiny ones who trust you for their care;
A lifetime spent discipling them's a lifetime pure and rare.
For when they put their hand in yours and know a daddy's love,
You're showing them a picture of the Father from above.

Look not toward worldly goal or gain or for your liberty;
Look only into their sweet eyes to find your ministry.
Devote your heart and sacrifice and make your manly mark—
There is none so great as he who finds his call as patriarch.

CHAPTER 9

THE RISE AND FALL AND RISE OF MOTHERHOOD IN AMERICA

Have We Forgotten that Only Women Can Be Mothers?

Only a woman can carry in her body an eternal being which bears the very image of God. Only she is the recipient of the miracle of life. Only a woman can conceive and nurture this life using her own flesh and blood and then deliver a living soul into the world. God has bestowed upon her alone a genuine miracle—the creation of life and the fusing of an eternal soul with mortal flesh. This fact alone establishes the glory of motherhood.

Despite the most creative plans of humanist scientists and lawmakers to redefine the sexes, no man will ever conceive and give birth to a child. The fruitful womb is a holy gift given by God to women alone. This is one reason why the office of wife and mother is the highest calling to which a woman can aspire.

This is the reason why nations that fear the Lord esteem and protect mothers. They glory in the distinctions between men and women and attempt to build cultures in which motherhood is honored and protected.

In his famous commentary on early American life, *Democracy in America*, Alexis de Tocqueville explained:

> *Thus the Americans do not think that man and woman have either the duty or the right to perform the same offices, but they show an equal regard for both their respective parts; and though their lot is different, they consider both of them as beings of equal value. They do not give to the courage of woman the same form or the same direction as to that of man, but they never doubt her courage; and if they hold that man and his partner ought not always to exercise their intellect and understanding in the same manner, they at least believe the understanding of the one to be as sound as that of the other, and her intellect to be as clear.*

De Tocqueville contrasted the American understanding of women with European sentiments:

> *There are people in Europe who, confounding together the*

different characteristics of the sexes, would make man and woman into beings not only equal but alike. They could give to both the same functions, impose on both the same duties, and grant to both the same rights; they would mix them in all things—their occupations, their pleasures, their business. It may readily be conceived that by thus attempting to make one sex equal to the other, both are degraded, and from so preposterous a medley of the works of nature nothing could ever result but weak men and disorderly women.

The War on Motherhood

America's glory was her women. De Tocqueville believed this when he wrote:

As for myself, I do not hesitate to avow that although the women of the United States are confined within the narrow circle of domestic life, and their situation is in some respects one of extreme dependence, I have nowhere seen woman occupying a loftier position; and if I were asked, now that I am drawing to the close of this work, in which I have spoken of so many important things done by the Americans, to what the singular prosperity and growing strength of that people ought mainly to be attributed, I should reply: To the superiority of their women.

But this birthright would be exchanged during the last

century for a mess of pottage. Perhaps the greatest legacy of the twentieth century has been the war on motherhood and biblical patriarchy. Feminists, Marxists, and liberal theologians have made it their aim to target the institution of the family and divest it from its biblical structure and priorities. The results are androgyny, a radical decline in birthrate, and a radical rise in abortion, fatherless families, and social confusion.

Incredibly, the biggest story of the twentieth century never made headline news [i]. Somehow we missed it. It was the mass exodus of women from the home, and the consequent decline of motherhood. For the first time in the recorded history of the West, more mothers left their homes than stayed in them. By leaving the home, the experience and reality of childhood, family life, and femininity were fundamentally redefined, and the results have been so bad that, if this one trend is not reversed, our grandchildren may live in a world where both the true culture of Christian family life and the historic definition of marriage are the stuff of fairy tales.

Many "isms" have influenced these trends—

---

[i] In his 2002 book, *Bias: A CBS Insider Exposes How the Media Distort the News,* Bernard Goldberg wrote: They don't report the really big story—arguably one of the biggest stories of our time— that is absence of mothers from American homes is without any historical precedent, and that millions upon millions of American children have been left, as Eberstadt puts it, "to fend for themselves—with dire consequences." Pg. 166

evolutionism, feminism, statism, eugenicism, Marxism, and more. But in the end, the philosophical gap between the presuppositions of the Atheists, eugenicists, and Marxists of the early twentieth century and the presuppositions of the professing Church in the twenty-first century, have narrowed dramatically. The goals of the state and the goals of the mainstream church have so merged, that the biblical family with its emphasis on male headship, generational succession, and prolific motherhood are a threat to the social order of both institutions.

Less than one hundred years ago, the architects of the atheistic communist Soviet state anticipated the death of the Christian family. They explained the need for destroying the Christian family with its emphasis on motherhood and replacing it with a vision for a "new family." Lenin wrote:

> We must now say proudly and without any exaggeration that apart from Soviet Russia, there is not a country in the world where women enjoy full equality and where women are not placed in the humiliating position felt particularly in day-to-day family life. This is one of our first and most important tasks... Housework is the most unproductive, the most barbarous and the most arduous work a woman can do. It is exceptionally petty and does not include anything that would in any way promote the development of the woman.... The

building of socialism will begin only when we have achieved the complete equality of women and when we undertake the new work together with women who have been emancipated from that petty, stultifying, unproductive work. . . . We are setting up model institutions, dining-rooms and nurseries, that will emancipate women from housework. . . . These institutions that liberate women from their position as household slaves are springing up where it is in any way possible... Our task is to make politics available to every working woman.

In his 1920 "International Working Women's Day Speech," Lenin emphasized:

The chief thing is to get women to take part in socially productive labor, to liberate them from 'domestic slavery,' to free them from their stupefying [idiotic] and humiliating subjugation to the eternal drudgery of the kitchen and the nursery. This struggle will be a long one, and it demands a radical reconstruction, both of social technique and of morale. But it will end in the complete triumph of Communism.

Lenin's comrade Trotsky played a key role in communicating the Marxist vision of what he called the "new family." Lenin and Trotsky believed in the overthrow of Christianity by destroying the biblical family. They sought to build a new state, free from historic

Christian presuppositions concerning the family. This meant denigrating the biblical notion of male headship and hierarchy within the family. It meant eliminating any sense that there should be a division of labor between man and wife. This required delivering women from the burdens of childbirth and childcare. It meant adopting tools like birth control as guarantors that women could be free to remain in the workforce. Trotsky said this:

> *Socialization of family housekeeping and public education of children are unthinkable without a marked improvement in our economics as a whole. We need more socialist economic forms. Only under such conditions can we free the family from the functions and cares that now oppress and disintegrate it. Washing must be done by a public laundry, catering by a public restaurant, sewing by a public workshop. Children must be educated by good public teachers who have a real vocation for the work. Then the bond between husband and wife would be freed from everything external and accidental, and the one would cease to absorb the life of the other. Genuine equality would at last be established....*

The most disturbing part of quotes like those above is how similar they sound in sentiment and spirit to voices today from individuals who claim to be a part of the Church of Jesus Christ. Even more disturbing is how many of the anti-family social reforms are presuppositions of modern Christians in America; presuppositions which have been fully accepted.

How America's Conscience Was Seared Toward Motherhood

But motherhood is not easily defeated. It was here from the beginning, and it has always carried the Church and civilization forward. Motherhood not only perpetuates civilization, it defines it.

At first, Jamestown was a bachelor society struggling for survival. But she became a civilization when the women arrived. Plymouth, on the other hand, began as a civilization—families of faith committed to fruitfulness and multiplication for the glory of God, an impossibility without motherhood.

Motherhood is not easily defeated because God has placed reminders of its importance in the very bodies of the women He created. To defeat motherhood, the enemies of the biblical family must do more than make it a social inconvenience; they must teach women to despise themselves by viewing their own wombs as the enemy of self-fulfillment. This means minimizing the glorious gift of life which is only given to womankind. It means redefining what it means to be a woman.

But even this is not enough. To defeat motherhood, the enemies of the biblical family must sear the conscience of an entire generation of women. This is done through the doctrines of social emancipation from the home, sexual liberation, birth control, and abortion—all four of which cause a woman to war against her created nature. Instead of being the blessed guardian of domesticity for society, she is taught that contentment can only be found by acting like, dressing like, and competing with men. Instead of being an object of respect, protection, and virtue, she sells herself cheaply, thus devaluing her womanhood. Instead of glorying in a fruitful womb, she cuts off the very seed of life. Sometimes she even kills the life.

Years of playing the part of a man hardens a woman. It trains women to find identity in the corporation, not the home. It teaches them to be uncomfortable around children and large families—the mere presence of which is a reminder of the antithesis between God's design for womankind and the norms of post-Christian societies.

But women are not the only ones with seared consciences. Men have them too. Consider that, fifty years ago, a man would have winced to think of female soldiers heading into combat while stay-at-home dads are left behind changing diapers. Today's man has a seared conscience. He no longer thinks of himself as a protector of motherhood and a defender of womankind. He comforts himself by repeating the mantras of modern feminism and by assuring himself of how reasonable and enlightened he is—how different he is from his intolerant and oppressive fathers. But in his heart, modern man knows that he has lost something. He has lost his manhood.

To be a man, you must care about women, and you must care about them in the right way. You must care about them as being worthy of protection, honor, and love. This means genuinely appreciating them for their uniqueness as women. It means recognizing the preciousness of femininity over glamour, of homemaking over careerism, and of mature motherhood over perpetual youth. But when women are reduced to soldiers, sexual objects, and social competitors, it is not merely the women who lose the identity given to them by the Creator, but the men as well. This is why the attack on motherhood has produced a nation of eunuchs—socially and spiritually impotent men who have little capacity to lead, let alone love women as God intended man to love woman—as mothers, wives, sisters, and daughters.

Motherhood Will Triumph

There is an important reason why motherhood will not be defeated—The Church is her guardian. As long as she perseveres—and persevere she will—motherhood will prevail.

The Church is the ultimate vanguard of that which is most precious and most holy. She holds the oracles of God which dare to proclaim to a selfish, self-centered nation:

Children are a blessing and the fruit of the womb is His reward. —Psalm 127:3

The Church stands at the very gates of the city, willing to receive the railing complaints of feminists, atheists, and the legions arrayed against the biblical family, and she reminds the people of God:

Let the older women teach the young to love their children, to guide the homes. —Titus 2:3-5

It is this very love of the life of children, this passion for femininity and motherhood, which may be God's instrument of blessing on America in the days to come. As the birth rate continues to plummet, divorce rates rise, and family life in America dissipates to the point of extinction, life-loving families will not only have an important message to share, but they will have an army of children to help them share it.

The Question:

Teacher: Susie, what do you want to be when you grow up?

Susie: I want to be a doctor.

Teacher: How wonderful! And what about you, Julie?

Julie: I want to be a soldier.

Teacher: How commendable! And what about you, Hannah?

Hannah: When I grow up I want to be a wife and mother!

Teacher: [dead silence]

After years of society belittling the calling of motherhood, something wonderful is happening—

something wonderfully counter-cultural! In the midst of the anti-life, anti-motherhood philosophies which pervade the culture, there is a new generation of young ladies emerging whose priorities are not determined by the world's expectations of them. They have grown up in homes where fathers shepherded them, where children are not merely welcome, but where they are deeply loved. Some of these women have been home educated, which means that many of them have grown up around babies and their mothers. They have learned to see motherhood as a joy and a high calling because their parents see it that way.

When asked about their future, these girls know their own minds. These are the future mothers of the Church: Young women who are not afraid to say that the goal of all of their education and training is to equip them to pursue the highest calling of womanhood—the office of wife and mother.

The Cost of Motherhood

Once a lady went to visit her friend. During the visit, the children of the friend entered the room and began to play with each other. As the lady and her friend visited, the lady turned to her friend and said eagerly, and yet with no evident thought to the meaning of her words:

"Oh, I'd give my life to have such children."

The mother replied, with a subdued earnestness whose quiet told of the depth of experience out of which her words came:

"That's exactly what it cost."

There is a cost of motherhood, and the price is no small sum. If you are not willing to pay this price, no amount of encouragement about the joys of motherhood will satisfy.

But the price of motherhood is not fundamentally different from the price of being a disciple of Jesus Christ. In fact, Christian mothers see their duty as mothers flowing from their calling to Jesus Christ. And what is this cost?

Christian motherhood means dedicating your entire life in service of others. It means standing beside your husband, following him, and investing in the lives of children whom you hope will both survive you and surpass you. It means foregoing present satisfaction for eternal rewards. It means investing in the lives of others who may never fully appreciate your sacrifice or comprehend the depth of your love. And it means doing all these things, not because you will receive the praise of man—for you will not—but because God made you to be a woman and a mother, and there is great contentment in that biblical calling.

In other words, motherhood requires vision. It requires living by faith and not by sight.

These are some of the reasons why motherhood is both the most biblically noble and the most socially unappreciated role to which a young woman can aspire. There are many people who ask the question: "Does my life matter?" But a mother that fears the Lord need never ask such a question. Upon her faithful obedience hinges the future of the Church and the hope of the nation.

In 1950, the great Scottish-American preacher, Peter Marshall, stood before the United States Senate and explained it this way:

> *The modern challenge to motherhood is the eternal challenge— that of being a godly woman. The very phrase sounds strange in our ears. We never hear it now. We hear about every other kind of women—beautiful women, smart women, sophisticated women, career women, talented women, divorced women, but so seldom do we hear of a godly woman—or of a godly man either, for that matter.*
>
> *I believe women come nearer fulfilling their God-given function in the home than anywhere else. It is a much nobler thing to be a good wife than to be Miss America. It is a greater achievement to establish a Christian home than it is to produce a second-rate novel filled with filth. It is a far, far better thing in*

the realm of morals to be old-fashioned than to be ultramodern. The world has enough women who know how to hold their cocktails, who have lost all their illusions and their faith. The world has enough women who know how to be smart. It needs women who are willing to be simple. The world has enough women who know how to be brilliant. It needs some who will be brave. The world has enough women who are popular. It needs more who are pure. We need women, and men, too, who would rather be morally right than socially correct.

May we remember that we are fighting for the Lord, and that it is He who prioritizes motherhood and home as the highest calling and domain of womanhood "that the word of God be not blasphemed" (Titus 2:5).

May the Lord fill our churches with faithful mothers.

CHAPTER 10

THE SINS OF
NELLIE OLESON

*Lessons in Rebellion from
"Little House on the Prairie"*

Now I want you to do your best to picture a scene that unfolded before my very eyes one summer evening a few years ago:

Nine members of the Phillips family are packed into the suburban and headed across America to home-sweet-home in Texas. We have just left an out-of-state home school convention where Daddy was a keynote speaker. Our minds are filled with thoughts of the new friends we had met and all we had learned at the conference.

It is now evening time. We are pooped after a long

day's driving. We snugly cram into our hotel room. Our children sleep on the floor or in beds (based on their age and size). I go to snuggle for a few minutes, talk to, and pray over my little girls.

Suddenly I notice something very odd: My six-year-old daughter Jubilee is lying down on her makeshift bed on the floor. Her nose is scrunched up. She is shaking her head and looking at the ceiling with great intensity.

"Jubilee, darling," says I. "What's troubling you?"

She looks at me with sustained intensity:

"Nellie Oleson is a wicked, sinful girl."

"Do you mean that Nellie Oleson who is a friend of Laura on *Little House on the Prairie?*"

"Oh Daddy, she is no friend to Laura," Jubilee declares. "She is a wicked, sinful little girl. Do you know what she did to Laura?"

I asked her to tell me.

Jubilee now proceeds to give me a blow-by-blow, episode-by-episode recounting of the rebellious behavior of Nellie—complete with Jubilee's own commentary from the Book of Proverbs on such behavior from the Bible.

Apparently, about a dozen episodes into the season, my three daughters had gotten together for a pow-wow. After some deliberation, they determined that Nellie Oleson was surely the naughtiest little girl who had ever been born. Ever!

After all, who could be more naughty than Nellie Oleson?

At this point, I noticed two other figures in nightgowns sneaking their way over to the cranny where Jubilee and I were having our dialogue.

Faith joins the conversation: "Nellie Oleson is a wicked little girl. She deserves twelve spankings, maybe even a million googleplex spankings." (Please don't think my little Faith is a sadist. This is just her way of translating what she hears from her Daddy's talk on biblical mathematics into her little girl vision of a remedy for an undisciplined child.)

"She gets to wear all the fancy dresses and have the fancy rings in her hair. And then she makes fun of poor girls like Laura," Faith exclaimed.

"And her momma is a mean woman, too," chimes in Liberty. "I think Mrs. Oleson is like Jezebel in the Bible because she bosses her husband."

"She's bossy," says Faith.

"Just like Nellie," says Jubilee.

"I like her daddy," said Liberty, "But he doesn't really lead his family."

Right about now, I am wondering if the *Little House on the Prairie* series should be on the "how to raise a discerning child" suggested curriculum list. In fairness, there are lots of problems with the *Little House on the Prairie* television show, but at this point I am thinking that the producers have done a masterful job of teaching children the principle, "as a jewel of gold in the snout of a swine, so is a beautiful woman that lacks discretion."

Come to think of it, I seem to remember being outraged by Nellie when I was a young teenager watching the show when it was first broadcast. (Though I think that, at the time, my solution for her bad attitude was a little less charitable and restrained than my daughters'. If I remember correctly, it had something to do with a pair of scissors and her golden locks, a pond of mud, her pretty dresses, and a good swift kick in the *tuchus*.)

And so it is, and so it ever shall be.

As long as our children and grandchildren and perhaps great-grandchildren journey back in time to the town of Walnut Grove and the world of a little girl named Laura Ingalls, that Nellie Oleson is and shall remain the quintessential example of a spoiled brat—the very personification to our little ones of what it means to grow up without a strong father and the loving, gracious, but timely, application of the rod of correction to one's posterior.

CHAPTER 11

OUR FATHERS' ROCK

Why We Must Not Remove
the Ancient Landmarks

Once considered the cradle of American democracy,
Plymouth is slowly but surely being transformed into a city
ashamed of its past.

If you find yourself standing in front of Plymouth Rock this Thanksgiving Day, do not expect to hear stories of pious Pilgrims in search of religious freedom. Before you go, prepare your children and family for a slightly different vision of America's past.

If you walk less than a hundred yards from Plymouth Rock and ascend to Cole's Hill, the magnificent burial ground of the fifty Pilgrims who perished during the first cold winter of 1620, you will not only encounter hundreds of demonstrators who gather on the last Thursday of every November to disabuse the memory of the Pilgrim fathers, but you can also read the new monument plaques that describe the devastating effect of Christianity on North America, the "genocide" of Native Americans by the Pilgrims and the importance of treating Thanksgiving as a "National Day of Mourning."

Once viewed by poets and politicians as the cradle of American democracy, Plymouth is gradually being transformed—a stunning example of how a few revisionist historians and a small cadre of well-organized political activists can pressure a community into renouncing its heritage.

In November of 1999, I unwittingly found myself an observer to one small but significant step toward this transformation. It was the day before Thanksgiving. Standing on Cole's Hill, I gathered my wife and four children around the great stone sarcophagus containing recovered bones of the Pilgrims who died during the first winter. Just a few yards to my left stood the towering statue erected in 1921 by the Improved Order of Red Men and dedicated to "Massasoit, the great sachem of the Wampanoags: Protector and Preserver of the Pilgrims." It commemorates the famed chieftain who adopted

Christian names for his children and who facilitated an unprecedented fifty-year treaty of unbroken peace between the local Indian community and the Pilgrim settlement.

Since it was to be the last Thanksgiving of the millennium, I determined that my children needed to know and understand the Pilgrim legacy. With the uncertainty of a new century before us, I wanted to take a special opportunity to exhort my sons and daughters to embrace a Pilgrim vision for dependence on God, for self-sacrifice, and for multigenerational faithfulness. I wanted to pray for them and over them at the place where American freedom began.

Few people realize our country was founded by a devout band of nonconformist Christians who lived and breathed a vision for family and community they understood to be clearly defined by the Bible. Though the Pilgrims left England because of religious persecution, they also left Holland for America for several other reasons.

Governor William Bradford, the Pilgrim leader, explains in *Of Plymouth Plantation* that they had multiple goals: to protect their children from ungodly peer influences of the culture in Holland, to bring the gospel to the natives, and to lay a foundation of multigenerational faithfulness for their children and a future society.

Bradford proclaimed that these families were more than willing to sacrifice their lives, if necessary—"even though they be but stepping stones"—for future generations of believers they would never meet.

Each of these goals was achieved: Many Indians were converted to Christ; generations of Pilgrims remained faithful to the vision and a nation was ultimately birthed, its charter documents drawing extensively from the principles of self-government and freedom under God communicated by the Mayflower Compact.

Remove Not the Ancient Landmarks

With this in mind, I had taken my family to Plymouth. On Cole's Hill, I asked God to make them mighty warriors for Christ with a rich multigenerational vision. I was just reminding my son of the text from Scripture—"remove not the ancient landmarks"—when a truck pulled up. Out of the truck came city workers carrying shovels. They began to dig just yards from where I stood. I approached them and engaged in a most unusual conversation:

"What are you digging?" I asked.

"We're placing a new monument marker for the city," they replied.

"May I see what's on it?"

"We aren't sure. We were just told to dig the hole. Someone else will put the marker in tonight."

"Now why would anyone put a marker on Cole's Hill under cover of darkness?"

"We aren't sure. We were just told to dig the hole."

Most revolutions are staged at night, so it should have been no surprise to discover the next day permanent stone markers and plaques in multiple locations around Plymouth, including Cole's Hill, which present Thanksgiving Day as a day of mourning over the invasion of this continent by thieving murderers.

Talk about historical schizophrenia. The "Pilgrim genocide" markers, on the exact spot 380 years ago that Pilgrims had buried their dead at night, are just a few yards from the great stone sarcophagus inscription at the Tercentenary, which reads:

Here under cover of darkness the fast dwindling company laid their dead, leveling the Earth above them lest the Indians should learn how many were their graves. Reader, history records no nobler venture for faith and freedom than that of this pilgrim band. In weariness and painfulness in watchings often in hunger and cold, they laid the foundations of a state wherein every man through countless ages should have liberty to worship God in his own way. May their example inspire

*thee to do thy part in perpetuating and spreading the lofty
ideals of our Republic throughout the world.*

The same forces of political correctness behind the
markers returned on Thanksgiving afternoon, as my
family did. Demonstrators (most of whom appeared to
be college students, not Native Americans) rejoiced over
their new victory by desecrating the other monuments,
including that of William Bradford and even Massasoit,
who some consider to have been a collaborator with the
Pilgrim enemy. For a man who had just traveled 1,500
miles to remember the faith of my spiritual fathers and to
introduce it to my children, this was truly heartbreaking.

I placed my children in the car with my wife, locked
the door, grabbed my Bible, walked to the new monument
and began to share some words of encouragement from
Scripture and from American history with the tourists
who were beginning to assemble. The response was less
than enthusiastic. After all, they had just read the plaque
and listened to "experts" offer the new revised version of
history. And if the town of Plymouth is finally officially
willing to get the message of Pilgrim genocide out, then
it must be true.

When things died down, I took my firstborn son
and walked to each monument defaced with obscenities

or littered with pagan paraphernalia. We relocated the material—into trash receptacles—and walked away to pray.

Rent a Riot

The genesis of the decision by the town of Plymouth to erect "National Day of Mourning/Genocide" plaques dates back to 1997, when a group calling itself the United American Indians of New England (UAINE) disrupted a historic march called The Pilgrim's Progress to stage a violent confrontation.

Since the 1920s, it had been the custom of the Mayflower Society to host a march through Plymouth commemorating the loss of the first fifty-one Pilgrims. The Pilgrim's Progress usually draws thousands of visitors, many in historic costume and some of whom are direct Mayflower descendants. The marchers walk through town to Burial Hill, where an authentic Pilgrim service is performed. The gospel witness of the service is distinctive—prayers, psalm-singing, and declarations of trust in Almighty God.

So who were these protesters and where did they come from? Four years later, the facts remain unclear. What is clear, however, is that the leaders of the protest specifically recruited participants, including members of radical out-of-state groups, with one goal in mind: to create a media event they could use as leverage against the town of Plymouth.

One of the marchers in the 1997 Pilgrim's Progress, who asked not to be identified, put it this way: "They needed to get some money for their agenda, and they knew the best way to do this was by creating a media frenzy, so they called 'rent a riot.'"

According to several participants in the 1997 march, protesters dressed as Indians surrounded the Pilgrims, blockaded them from proceeding, and threatened them. At least one marcher was assaulted. When police intervened, the protesters resisted, making sure to behave in a way that would facilitate later charges of police impropriety against Native Americans.

The media had a field day. National newspapers declared new tension between Indians and Pilgrims. The result? Plymouth allowed the protesters a regular Thanksgiving Day forum near Plymouth Rock and to erect new markers across Plymouth designed to communicate the "genocide" perspective of Pilgrim history.

But is any of it true? Is the American dream built upon a lie? Shouldn't fair-minded Christians feel a twinge of guilt before tasting that turkey? After all, if our spiritual forefathers committed atrocities, shouldn't we be willing to fess up to the facts?

Ask a growing number of scholars and historians about those facts, and they won't hesitate to defend the Pilgrim colonists.

"Most of these charges against the Pilgrims are based on pop history, not historical analysis," says Paul Jehle, the education director of the Plymouth Rock Foundation, a nonprofit organization founded during the 350th anniversary of the Plymouth settlement.

Jehle rattles off the many dates, names, charters, and deeds that make up the rich legacy of Pilgrim and Indian relations. He points out that Indian and Pilgrim communities alike benefited from cross-cultural contact. Pilgrims not only introduced economic principles of free trade to the Indians, allowing them to prosper financially, but they helped the Indians redeem mineral-depleted land using the Old Testament laws of crop rotation. Similarly, without Indian knowledge of innovative ways to fertilize crops in the harsh New England soil, the Pilgrims would have failed. Each culture was advanced by coming into contact with the other.

The greatest benefit of Pilgrim contact with the Indians was the introduction of the gospel. Through the foundation laid by the Pilgrims and continued later by men like twentieth-century martyr Jim Elliot, many thousands—even whole tribes—were converted to Christ. In fact, by 1670 the entire Indian population of Martha's Vineyard Island was converted. Many of these Christian "praying Indians" remained faithful and actually took up arms on behalf of the colonists during the bloody season known as Prince Phillip's War.

Not Guilty

So what about the charges of genocide, theft, and ill will by the Pilgrims against the natives?

- The charge that Pilgrims stole the land from the natives is false. Pilgrim leaders viewed it as a moral and legal obligation to contract for the purchase of lands with the Wampanoag, with whom they entered into land deeds and signed covenants. Nothing was stolen. Western and biblical concepts of property ownership were not recognized by the local population during the Christian settlement. In the pantheistic worldview of Indian culture, the land belonged to everyone and to nature itself.

- The claim that Pilgrims committed genocide against the Indian tribes is false; the precise opposite is true. For more than fifty years, Pilgrims and local Indians lived in a state of equanimity and peace. Because Indian tribes constantly warred with one another, the Pilgrims found themselves on at least one occasion acting in military concert with the Wampanoag in standing against invading tribes, but such an action was in self-defense—a far cry from genocide.

- The claim that the Pilgrim community lived in a state of tension and enmity with the Wampanoag is false. The official Pilgrim policy was to treat the Indian tribes as sovereign foreign states. In the case of the Wampanoag, this meant they were afforded all the legal rights and respect due any foreign power.

As Jehle observes, Indian tribes often were treated improperly by later groups of European settlers not bound by the strict code of Christian conduct and law to which the Pilgrims subscribed, but the Plymouth community stands out as a model example of the "right way" to interact with a native population.

A Faithful Remnant

It's easy to look at the new, historically inaccurate and politically motivated monuments now standing near Plymouth Rock and feel defeated. But more than a little hope can be found in the story of another monument, the most magnificent and prominent historical marker in the town.

Back in 1989, a Plymouth council had convened to determine the fate of the Founders' Monument. The colossal structure, completed in 1889, stands eighty-one feet tall and was designed to communicate the Pilgrim ideals of faith, morality, education, law, liberty, and justice.

The monument was complete and perfect in every respect but one. For more than one hundred years, one side had remained uninscribed, primarily because no one could decide what should be written on it.

Fearing that some future generation might be less generous with the Pilgrim legacy, Jehle moved to have a quote from Bradford etched on the stone tablet. The motion was doomed, except for one small fact. Seated in the audience that day, for the first time ever, was an octogenarian from Florida named Verna Orndorff, well known for her generous patronage, who had flown in to attend her first and last meeting.

Jehle read the Bradford quote:

Thus out of small beginnings greater things have grown by His hand Who made all things out of nothing, and gives being to all things that are; and as one small candle may light a thousand, so the light kindled here has shone to many, yea, in a sense, to our whole nation; let the glorious name of Jehovah have all the praise.

With tears in her eyes, the elderly Mrs. Orndorff declared:

My father had me memorize this quote when I was a little girl. . . . If you will vote for it, I will pay for it.

The great quote is now etched on the monument and stands as an ever-present reminder to every one of the estimated thirty-five million physical descendants of the fifty people who survived the first winter, as well as to an entire nation that owes its gratitude to those first settlers. The message? That few visions have ever been as beautifully realized as that embraced by this ragtag band of devoted moms and dads.

This article appeared in *Citizen* magazine. Copyright © 2001 Focus on the Family. All rights reserved. International copyright secured.

CHAPTER 12

WATCHING OUR SWEETHEARTS GROW UP

The Beauty and Pain of Having Daughters

A s we have done each year on her birthday, Jubilee and I spent a day together telling stories, eating at *la Madeleine,* taking pictures, and simply having a grand time.

Jubilee can be a rootin'-tootin' cowgirl or a girlie-girl, depending on her mood. For the last two years, she has decided that the latter was the spirit *du jour* for her birthday. Appropriately, she donned a favorite dress—her vintage *Titanic* outfit—and showed up on the morning of her birthday at my bedroom door to announce that she was ready for her day with Daddy.

Some things are just too beautiful for words. One of them is a little girl that longs to be in the presence of her father.

"Daddy, can we go out for our tea time now?"

Wait a minute. Wasn't it just yesterday that we celebrated her last birthday, and she wore the same dress, and said the very same words to me? The dress fits her differently this year, and the raspy, childish voice I knew so well has been replaced by the voice of a young lady. When did that happen?

Is she really six years old? She is so beautiful.

Right about now, I feel that deep, deep sinking feeling of wonder, awe, and helplessness. Yes, real helplessness. I desperately want to hold onto something that is beyond my grasp—something that I am not meant to hold forever.

Oh Lord, just one more decade to hold that tiny hand. Please Father, just a little more time to live with and love the little girl whose dolly is never far from her arms and who longs to be in her father's arms. Just a few more decades of birthdays, bathed in the unfathomable devotion and unfeigned innocence of the little girl before me.

I know it is the sacred duty of every father to bring his daughter into noble, womanly maturity, and wedlock. Each season is precious. I know this. I have preached it.

But at this moment, this emotional moment, I simply want her to remain the little girl with the pink *Titanic* dress, the bowed hat, and the dolly in her arms forever.

Is that so much to ask?

I know the answer, of course, but it does not seem to bring resolution to the heart of a father that aches for his precious one.

But there is one thought that quickly brings me back to reality: My time with my children is a gift from God. He owns my time, and He owns my children. As much as I love them, He loves them and me more. The very fact that I have the capacity to love my daughter is evidence that I am made in the image of God. Compared to God's love, my love is nothing.

How the Father must love His own children—such unfathomable, unsurpassed love.

Yes, it is hard watching our sweethearts grow up. But it is also beautiful. And this pain in my heart, this fatherly ache, drives home the fact that I must number my days and drink deeply from every opportunity to live and to love the little girl in the pink dress while God yet gives me opportunity.

> *That our sons may be as plants grown up in their youth;*
> *that our daughters may be as corner stones, polished after the*
> *similitude of a palace.* —Psalm 144:12